Forgotten Christian

by Nancy L. Walker

This book is dedicated to all the valiant warriors on the front lines in the battle for life!

Acknowledgements

With a grateful heart I wish to thank:

The dear sisters and brothers in the Lord who made this book possible.

Pastor Fred whose godly actions and example has been, and always will be, an inspiration to many.

Pastor Paul, my brother in the Lord, for his confidence in me.

My children, who are the sweetness of my life.

My grandchildren, who have humbled me, in their love for Jesus and willingness to join me on the front lines.

Thank you, readers of this book in your willingness to walk with us in this word picture.

Most of all, to Jesus my Christ, who saved me from my wicked ways. He holds me in His loving arms, never leaves me and fills me with His Love!

The Forgotten Christian

Bible Used

Unless otherwise indicated, all Scripture quotations are taken from the New International Version (NIV)

ISBN 1-59919-034-6

PUBLISHED BY

Elim Publishing

Lima, NY

Table of Contents

Introduction

"Rescue those being led away to death; hold back those staggering toward slaughter. If you say, "But we knew nothing about this," does not He who weighs the heart perceive it? Does not He who guards your life will know it? Will He not repay each person according to what he has done?"
(Proverbs 24:11-12)

From all points of communication, we are bombarded with negative and false information. The media, the government, the educational system, and even some churches have an incorrect concept of who, why, and what an on-the-street pro-life Christian activist/missionary is.

When is the last time you have heard your Pastor say the following from the pulpit: "This week because of the faithfulness of the Christians on the street, five babies were saved from abortion, three people accepted Christ as Savior, two cribs were supplied for moms and over 200 tracts were given away. Let us all rejoice in the Lord for their steadfastness and join them in prayer and support."? I venture to say some who read this have never heard that statement from their Pastor.

This is the untold story of victories, of salvations, of heartbreaks, and of Christians who have gone to jail for life and for Jesus in our own country. This is the truth of what really happens day after day at the local abortion centers in the United States.

"You did not choose Me, but I chose you and appointed you to go and bear fruit—fruit that will last." (John 15:16a)

Or as the old saying goes, "the proof is in the pudding." It is my heart's desire that this word picture of the "direct action pro-life Christian" will be proof that standing up for Christ and life at the abortion centers not only bears fruit, but fruit that lasts.

There are four assigned positions on any given day at the local abortion centers:

Sidewalk counselors are Christians dedicated to passing out information on fetal development and complications from abortion, along with telephone numbers of crisis pregnancy centers who offer care, long or short term.

Then there is the ***prayer warrior***. Prayer warriors are the Christians who focus strictly on praying at the centers. They intercede for the parents, the babies, counselors, abortionists and the people just walking by.

The ***sign bearers*** are the brave people that hold the signs for all to see. The message is always strong and true.

Last, but surely not least, are the ***camera person***. There have been so many false allegations regarding pro-life action on the street. These people are the protectors of the truth.

As sidewalk counselors, prayer warriors, sign bearers and camera person, we have been privileged to share the love of Jesus, share the truth and offer assistance to the moms going in, the workers, the abortionists, the dads and the grandparents. To have the opportunity to bear witness to our Lord's love to all who have walked by where we stand, is an honor. Some of these warriors have been standing for life for many years and have not grown weary.

You will read about *rescues*. These rescues took place in the late eighties and early nineties. This was when we would sit in front of the doors of an abortion center and stop the moms from going in. The police would come and drag us away. We were non-violent and in constant prayer that babies would be saved and our Lord would have mercy on the moms and dads. There were always sidewalk counselors there to help them in any way. Many Christians went to jail for doing this. Yet it was so worth it because abortion was exposed for what it really is and many babies were saved, moms were helped and we know the Lord was pleased. It is said that politicians don't see the light until they feel the heat. Well, we were God's fire and it lit the truth across our nation.

We are continually learning how to truly lean on Jesus and depend on Him for everything. We have seen Christians grow in Christ as they take a stand for Him. We have seen the unsaved saved, and the homosexual freed from sin. We have witnessed babies saved; miracles take place that blew our minds and the grace of God become more than sufficient. We have seen and are seeing the Holy Spirit's power, wisdom, and direction in the most incredible way. Mother's minds would not be changed without the Holy Spirit moving on their hearts. Our words are without power apart from the Lord's Spirit!

We have held the fruit of our labor: new born babies, mothers healed from the wounds of abortion, mothers who chose life for their children, brothers and sisters who have accepted Jesus as Lord and felt His forgiving love. We have held the horror of our apathy; the torn body of an aborted baby, the women in prison who were lost, addicted and prostituting themselves because of the abortion they had as a teenager. No one ever told them that Jesus loves them, forgives them and will give them a new start. We have held the weeping father because he could not save his baby. We have cried with the grandmothers who could not stop their young daughters from taking the life of their grandchild.

This book is the story of the "forgotten Christian." It is about the Christians who are His arms, legs, and eyes and who go, in the name of Jesus, where others will not. This is their story of victories, heartbreak, joy and grief.

The love that is shared on the *street* between the Christians is awesome, special and unique. The breakdown of denominational barriers to become His body, united in one purpose, is miraculous! Our drive is this: "Jesus is Lord, women are being exploited and injured, babies are being killed and fathers are being forgotten." It is a glorious testimony of what united love in Christ can do!

I know Christians who have been alongside me on the street whom I love dearly and would do anything for and I don't even know their last name. They are the pro-life Christian Samaritans that stop at the roadside and show compassion.

We have been persecuted by the world, the church, and our families and through it all we have grown in our faith; we will never give up being His ambassadors of love.

The miracles that take place are a powerful testimony of our Lord's mercy and grace. The fact that His saving grace is effective in front of the devil's workshops is the confirmation of His truth. The lives that have been and are being changed are the unquestionable witnesses to the working of the Holy Spirit.

The purpose of this book is to glorify Jesus Christ and to share with our fellow Americans just what we are all about. It is to answer the questions of:

- ***What does it feel like when there is a save?***
- ***What do the women who are going in think of us?***
- ***What of the fathers?***
- ***The grandparents?***
- ***The friends?***
- ***Why are we willing to go to prison for standing in front of an abortion center?***
- ***And . . . will it ever change?***

All of the testimonies in this book are actual stories. They have been compiled through a survey taken from over one hundred pro-lifers across the entire United States. Only first names are used for obvious reasons and because only our Lord receives the glory and honor. Jesus knows what is being done; He is pleased in what we do and He will give out the reward. In that truth we all rejoice!

Dear Lord, let this book be an encouragement to the "veteran warrior," an inspiration to the "rookie" and let it be used to touch the hearts of the people across this country! Amen

Chapter 1

Those Peculiar People

I thought I knew Jesus until I enlisted in His army and went to battle. Then I met Him face to Face!

"Who gave Himself for us that He might redeem us from all iniquity, and purify unto Himself a peculiar people, zealous of good works." (Titus 2:14 KJV)

It's Sunday morning in the year of 1987 and our church is full. The final song of worship has ended and it is now time for announcements. Lynn stands up again, it is the third Sunday in a row that this lady has stood in front of the congregation. "Is there anyone here who will give a few hours a week to go stand in front of an abortion center in town? We need you to give information to the women going into the center. You could save the life of a baby and help a lost woman by doing this!"

Everyone in church knows that abortion is wrong but they don't do much more than that. "Do I have a few hours to give? Will it do any good? And furthermore, I've already gone to several pro-life marches, isn't that enough?" I reasoned with myself. The first two weeks it was easy to dismiss Lynn's heartfelt request. This time it was not. I do have a few hours to give and what if I could change a mother's mind? Sharon in the next row felt the same way. We decided we would commit to one day a week for two hours.

It was Monday morning and we arrived at the abortion center. We've never been to one and we were pretty nervous. Lynn told us, "All you do is hand the information to the women going in." Sounded pretty easy. It was not! Both of us had read the pamphlets and at least knew what we were giving the women. The pamphlets had information on fetal development, complications from abortion and the alternatives that were available. Seemed to us these women would want this information before going in. Yet we realized how little we knew about abortion, complications, fetal development and so much more.

We felt pretty inadequate in our approaching the women. We prayed, "Father, guide, direct and speak through us in Jesus' name. Amen."

The first woman arrived, our hearts were pounding, our stomachs were jumping and it was amazing how much fear filled us at that moment of time. No words came out; we held out the literature and the woman just walked by and went in. Dumbfounded, we just stood there and then the realization fell upon us. *Conviction*: overcome by argument or proof. That mother had a living child within her which was going to be torn apart! My God, what is going on in there? Strange, isn't it? How we know something and then there comes a moment in time when that knowledge becomes active in our spirit and we perceive with certainty!

Another woman arrives, then another and another. Soon there were fifteen women in this place of horror. No one listened; no one took the pamphlets, they all just walked by us. We were fools, ignorant of the facts, overcome by fear and insecure about our ability. Then it was over. Our two hours of volunteer service was done for the week. In hushed tones we quietly said good-bye to each other and drove away. Life from that point took a drastic right turn!

Conviction comes in stages. Most of us "radicals" will say: "We knew we had to do something, and going is the first step." Four words of incredible intensity found in the Word of God are *love, give, go,* and *do*! Small words yet dynamic in their meaning.

Let me put it this way: "I Love God enough to Give of myself to Go and Do His will!"

After that dark Monday I knew I had to educate myself in the matter of abortion. Shock, guilt, revulsion, grief and confusion filled me as I went on to learn about fetal development and what the abortion procedures were. Studying the complications, I was astounded at how many there were. However, what infuriated me the most was the fact that the abortionist knew exactly what he/she was doing; they were taking the life of a human being! Their god is money. When I first started in the pro-life arena of activism it was 1987 and most of the women going for abortions were truly ignorant of the facts. It is now 2007, and most women know exactly what they are doing. Much truth has come to light recently regarding the facts on human development. Yet, back then the women were lied to, and because they perceived their situation to be unsolvable, they chose abortion.

I asked myself, "Where was I when this all started? How could I have been so deceived? What kind of game had I played with myself by believing if it is legal it must be right?"

The Scripture, "My people are destroyed from lack of knowledge," (Hosea 4:6a) took on a whole new meaning!

Lies create a cage, "only Truth will set you free!"

I believed the lie. I trusted the Supreme Court. Abortion was only being done in the beginning stages of pregnancy, when it was only tissue. You see, the problem is that in our society, the *cage* is very comfortable and *truth* is very uncomfortable and dangerous. It is much easier to believe the lie and delude ourselves. It's just like the classic science experiment with the frog in the water. That little ol' frog was very comfortable in the warm water. He just didn't *feel* the water heating up until it was too late, and then he was dead!

Truth was setting me free and boy was I uncomfortable. As I studied Scriptures on the shedding of innocent blood, the effects of abortion upon the mom and all the rest of it, a fire ignited in my heart that still burns intensely. I am sharing with you my own experience here, however, I know that so many other Christians have felt the same metamorphosis in their lives.

Those of us who go to the abortion centers around the United States (and the world for that matter) have, of our own free will, made the choice to be obedient to the Father and care enough about other human beings to put action to our convictions.

"Then I [we] heard the voice of the Lord saying, "Whom shall I send? And who will go for us?" And I [we] said, "Here am I. send me!" (Isaiah 6:8)

Does it hurt to go? Yes. However, we have learned that the more you know about what really goes on in the *legal* death chambers, the weaker the excuses not to go become.

Obedience to the Word of God and the prompting of the Holy Spirit equals an intimate relationship with Jesus that goes beyond anything we have asked or even thought about!

Faith becomes action. The more we exercise our faith the stronger it becomes. Yielding to the Lord's love and compassion produces effective results that saves lives and leads people to Him!

So we go, and in the going we learn, very quickly. We learn to lean on Jesus for direction, protection and guidance. Logic doesn't work. If it did abortion would definitely be illegal by now. The only action that produces results is the movement and mercy of the Father through His Holy Spirit! We have learned that it has to be His Word, His compassion, and His love through us that moves the hearts of the moms going in. Because of this truth, our walk with the Lord and our talk with the Lord has to be real and fully trusting. We pray to Him before we go, "Help us, protect us." We pray through Him while we are at the centers, "Use us, speak through us." And we pray in Him when we leave, "we did the best we could Lord, have mercy and move these moms to truth." The burden is too heavy when we leave, so we put it at the foot of the Cross.

The sidewalk counselors, prayer warriors, sign bearers, and camera people are a minority in the Christian community. For the most part their work for the Lord is completely ignored and, therefore, misunderstood. Very few Pastors, church members or family members ask, "How did it go today?" or "Can I pray for you today?" For some of us that's ok because it pushes us into the loving arms of Jesus. But for others the rejection is heartbreaking and pushes them right out of what the Lord has called them to do.

There is no doubt in my mind that if Jesus were physically here on earth today, He would be standing with us at the abortion centers. We truly know His Holy Spirit is there or we could not do what we do. Nor would we see the victories we do, if it were not for His Presence with us.

Another amazing change takes place when we stand for the Lord and life at the abortion centers. Within our spirits a determination and a curiosity evolved regarding other issues. Eyes to see and ears to hear are quickly developed. I will never forget one lady in particular. She was a registered nurse who knew abortion was the taking of a human life and was totally against it. Lucy joined us to counsel the moms at of the local abortion centers. She did not know Jesus as her Savior and Lord at first. After hanging around with us for a while and seeing His love in us, she accepted His love and forgiving grace. After that, Lucy became so burdened for mankind that she gave up everything and is now in Romania on the mission field!

For many, "going" is the spring board for so many other different mission fields. I am not out there as much as I used to be. I'm still there, yet not as much. The Lord has led me to teach children the truth about Him and life so they'll never go to an abortion center. When we are obedient to His direction we can depend upon Him to lead us where we should go! It is no longer just church on Sunday but Christianity as a way of life. I know for a fact that so many of the missionaries out there doing God's work started out by "going out" for life!

It's 5:30 in the morning, the alarm goes off and it is time to get up, fire up and go to the local abortion center. Do we want to go? No. Do we enjoy going? No! Will we go? Yes.

Yes, there are days when Christians go to the abortion centers and the battle is so intense, the moms going in totally hostile, the heartbreak extreme in degree, and not a victory in sight.

Then there are days when two, three, four moms change their minds, choose life for their child, and thank us for being there. There are days when a man walking down the street stops, listens and accepts Jesus as Savior of his life. They are days of glorious triumph!

As stated earlier, this is a word picture of the "forgotten Christian." One of the questions asked on the survey I mentioned was; "What has taking a visible stand at the abortion centers done for you in your personal life? Tell the happy and the sad."

The following is a composite of the responses:

The Happy:

"The Word of God became alive and active as I pressed on in the battle for life."

"Being active on the street has given me a sense of completion in Him."

"There are endless opportunities to witness the Gospel of Jesus Christ by being at the abortion centers."

"I've learned what intercessory prayer is all about. So many times we stand in front of the abortuaries and someone will drive by and yell an obscenity or make an obscene gesture and that became the signal to pray for them. To learn how to pray for the hostile stranger showing their anger has been an awesome lesson, not easily learned. Yet it was a teaching that has caused my love for Jesus to grow like none other. To see the lost through His eyes and to have the chance to stand in prayer for them has become a wonderful experience."

"Standing up for the little ones who cannot speak for themselves, offering the love of Jesus along with practical help for women in crisis has strengthened my faith like nothing else in my life."

"By being obedient to the command given to us in the Bible to "go" and asking our Lord to have His eyes to see, His ears to hear and His heart to feel has increased my love for others in a miraculous way!"

> *"Therefore, my beloved brethren, be steadfast, immovable, always abounding in the work of the Lord, knowing that your toil is not in vain."*
> *(1 Corinthians 15:58, ASV)*

"Any doubt about Jesus, His Word and being obedient to Him were removed when I took an active stand for the sanctity of life. I learned how unique each of us is and how much God loves us all. That lesson has spilled into my personal life and I have learned to appreciate my own life and realize how special I am to the Lord. We love because He first loved us. I have learned to look at my own family through His eyes and appreciate them so much more than I ever did!"

"Making a commitment to being at the abortion center to sidewalk counsel has increased my understanding of what a real commitment to Jesus Christ is all about."

"I have learned what real patience is. When a pro-abortion person starts to mock me, I've learned to be patient and keep my mouth shut. When a mom doesn't want to listen to the truth, I've learned to be silent and pray. When I get home and no one wants to hear about what happened that day I've learned to be humble and just give it to Jesus.

> *"Consider it pure joy, my brothers, whenever you face trials of many kinds, because you know that the testing of your faith develops perseverance. Perseverance must finish its work so that you may be mature and complete, not lacking anything."*
> *(James 1:2-4)*

"For me, being with Christians of the 'same mind' has been a blessing beyond measure. Lasting and loving bonds of friendship have been created in Christ by our working together with one purpose. I see what the Bible means when it says,

> *"If you have any encouragement from being united with Christ, if any comfort from His love, if any fellowship with the Spirit, if any tenderness and compassion, then make my joy complete by being like-minded, having the same love, being one in spirit and purpose. Do nothing out of selfish ambition or vain conceit, but in humility consider others better than yourselves. Each of you should look not only to your own interests, but also to the interests of others." (Philippians 2:1-4)*

"As a prayer warrior at the local abortion centers, I have learned that Scripture in the Bible that states in **Hebrews 13: 5b-6: "Never will I leave you; never will I forsake you"** So we say with confidence, "The Lord is my helper; I will not be afraid. What can man do to me?" is so absolutely true. There have been so many times when my brothers and sisters in Christ have told me that I am wrong for going to pray at these centers. And while I am there, the pro-abort people mock me, the cars driving by have splashed me, the people walking by have spit at me, the moms have screamed at me and through it all I always felt the presence of the Holy Spirit, and was filled with His wonderful peace. I always know that He is pleased with my obedience and is answering my prayers in His way and His time."

"But I tell you: Love your enemies and pray for those who persecute you." (Matthew 5:44a)

"When I first started to take a visible stand against abortion I was afraid to say anything. Then I found **Ps. 138:3, 'When I called, you answered me; you made me bold and stouthearted.'** Now you can't shut me up!"

"It is amazing how the Holy Spirit gives me the right words to say. He knows the mom and the baby that I am speaking to. I don't. Trusting the Holy Spirit to speak through me has saved many children and turned the hearts of the moms toward Jesus."

"All the things I've learned on how to battle at the abortion centers, all the Scriptures that I now know because of my decision to go, have become beneficial in my personal life. I now can cope with and have compassion on and in so many other areas of my life."

"You see that his faith and his actions were working together, and his faith was made complete by what he did." (James 2:22)

"Serving God in the direct action pro-life arena has increased my faith, increased my knowledge and if I hadn't made the decision to 'go' my grandchild would not be alive today!"

"To be instrumental in turning a woman away from aborting her child, to be able to help her, love her and bring her into the Kingdom of God is the most awesome blessing a Christian can ask for!"

"Love never fails." (1 Corinthians 13:8a)

The testimonies you have just read are profound, powerful and productive. Fruit grown in action is solid and remains. However, sometimes the cost can be very high. Read on.

The Sad:

"Remember the old saying, 'Make new friends but keep the old…'? Well, it just doesn't hold true when you decide to go against the 'mainstream'. Every old friend I had is gone. They think I'm crazy, too radical on and on. That hurts my heart."

"I go to my church on Sunday and no one talks to me. Everyone is sick of me asking them to go to the abortion center with me. No one ever asks how it was on the street or even is willing to pray for the babies with me. I don't understand, it is so clear to me, why can't they see too?"

"If I don't pray and prepare myself before I go to sidewalk counsel the spiritual warfare really does me in."

"For our struggle is not against flesh and blood, but against the rulers, against the authorities, against the powers of this dark world and against the spiritual forces of evil in the heavenly realms." (Ephesians 6:12)

"Seeing parents take their young daughters into the abortions center really breaks my heart."

"I cannot understand why the church at large does not stand up and show up as the body of Christ to end this killing!"

"Being 'out' there has made me realize how hard-hearted the men and women have become and it has convicted me of how far we have gone from being His light and salt in this dying land."

"I get really frustrated when the pro-aborts break the law and never get arrested. Yet there have been many times I have been arrested for walking onto the public parking lot to give information to a mom going in. And the worst part of that is my fellow Christians think I am the one who has done wrong!"

"My heart breaks when I see a fellow Christian get angry and argue with the pro-abort people."

"Seeing a woman go in anyway, after I've talked to her and told her the truth is very difficult for me."

"I have a real hard time dealing with the pro-abort people in a compassionate way. Especially when they take all the information that I give the moms away from them. They do not want these women to know the truth and know there is much help available. This really upsets me."

"The state of denial that exists in our country today just short circuits my brain."

"When we first started to be in front of the abortion centers in our community and the pro-abortion people mocked, swore, pushed, spit on us, it was devastating. In the beginning we felt like they hated us and that hurts. Especially because we are out there in love and have a real desire to help our fellow human beings. However, we have learned that they do not hate us but what and Whom we stand for and compassion for them enters our hearts!"

You have just read the happy and sad testimonies of what happens to us when we make the commitment to go. Through it all we grow, learn and draw closer to our King!

Everyone wants approval and the reactions that are evident at the abortion centers are extremely painful. I don't think anyone can be truly prepared for what happens when one takes a visible stand at a place where the lives of innocent babies are destroyed; at a place where moms are exploited for financial gain and fathers, in many instances, are just forgotten.

In training the sidewalk counselors, the prayer warriors and sign bearers, we share that hurtful experiences will occur. The Word says, **"Bless those who persecute you… and do not curse." (Romans 12:14)** However, when it happens you, well… Without His Holy Spirit to fill us with His love and give us His ability to see these people as He does, praying for them and loving them is truly impossible.

The word *persecute* means, "to harass or annoy persistently, to oppress because of one's religion, beliefs or race" (Noah Webster) In Greek it means to stand and suffer while someone is trying to drive you out. These are very good definitions of how the persecution is at the local abortion centers!

First of all, very few people want to see us out there. The moms don't want us there because we show them the truth and activate their conscience. The church does not want us there because we are exposing the sin of silence for all to see. The secular world does not want us there because our presence causes conviction to come upon them and that is "uncomfortable." The abortionist and their employees do not want us there because we expose their filthy deeds that are being committed for financial greed. No one wants us there except the Lord Jesus Christ! And that is enough for us to go.

In Isaiah 1:17 the Lord commands us to, "Learn to do right! Seek justice, encourage the oppressed. Defend the cause of the fatherless, plead the case of the widow." According to Strong's Concordance the Hebrew the word *defend* means "vindicate, contend, avenge and plead." Clearly, we can readily agree that there is no one more fatherless than a pre-born baby! We can easily understand that we ought to offer the mother in crisis help, love and the Gospel of Jesus.

Again, in James 1:27, "Religion that God our Father accepts as pure and faultless is this: to look after orphans and widows in their distress and to keep oneself from being polluted by the world." The Old Testament command is reaffirmed in the New. "Look after," according to Strong's Concordance in Greek means to go, see, relieve. It seems to us that "go, see, relieve" means we should go, see and relieve!

Therefore, we go and the persecution, the humiliation, the rejection and the heartbreak becomes a polishing cloth in the Hands of our Lord; used to clean us and shine us until we become transparent and only the Son can be seen. Glory to the King!

Our Lord sees our hearts; He is not concerned with the outward actions if the inward motivations are not pure. Are we there because we love the Lord, the moms, the dads, the babies? Are we really willing to suffer the hardships for the preciousness of life and the salvation of souls?

In our Lord's parable of the sower found in Matthew 13 we can draw some interesting observations for today's struggle for life.

Some people go to the abortion centers under real conviction, but the worries of the world cause them to fall away. Some go just to say they did but as soon as the persecution begins they are gone. Some go but the fear of man and the presence of death drives them away. But the ones who are convicted, determined and steadfast are testifying within this book that the Lord is pleased, babies are saved, souls are saved, people are helped and His light can shine on the hill!

It is not easy to loose friends, be mocked, spit on and given a cold shoulder in our churches and families; it is difficult to be lied about in the media and misunderstood by most everywhere by most everyone. No one wants to get up at five in the morning in the middle of winter to go to the abortion center week after week, month after month, year after year. It is heartbreaking to see dozens, no, thousands of babies being carried to their death. It is tragic to see the "empty mom" come out vomiting in the parking lot, hardly able to walk and no longer confident that abortion was the solution to the problem. No one enjoys standing in sub-zero weather or in the sizzling heat for hours at a time.

There were years when there were clinic defenders at the centers determined to stop us from telling the truth. They were extremely offensive especially when the homosexual "clinic defenders" did sexual things right in front of us to make us want to leave. It was tough to be arrested under false charges, convicted in an unjust court and sent to prison for loving and caring about our fellow human beings. Our faith was tested when the pro-aborts pushed us away from a mom who was just ready to change her mind, and take the information from her hands, tear her away and push her in the door.

In the area where we go, the clinic defenders are no longer there but when they were it was very tough!

It is not fun to have cars or buses try to run us over, have people drive by in the rain and deliberately splash us. It is difficult to have the mothers who are going into the centers become so violent from their guilt that they threaten our lives. The guards constantly bully us and the police are always trying to intimidate it up.

Is it worth it? Absolutely! I believe it is perfectly clear to everyone, especially Christians, that the legalization of child killing was wrong. Furthermore, we, the church, need to recognize the consequences of our silence. The body of Christ could have influenced our government not to legalize abortion. Aren't we His light bearers, responsible for bringing His light to this dark world?

Therefore, we have the responsibility to do all we can to offer the love of Jesus and assistance, in any way, to the mom who has been misled by the world's lies. We must do all we can to save the life of the little one who is just as special as you and I are and has just as much purpose and right to life as we do.

The Lord meets us at the abortion centers each time we are there. His Holy Spirit guides and directs our actions, our words, and our hearts. You will see in this book the miracles that only He alone can perform. The more we are determined to go the closer our relationship with Him becomes.

Taking a stand at the abortion center is a most difficult, heart wrenching ministry. Yet we obey, we go, we cry, we laugh, we are misunderstood, we are forgotten by our brethren, but never by our Lord and we rejoice in the privilege of serving Him! We truly are a peculiar people!

"Blessed Assurance, Jesus is mine!"
This is my [our] story, this is my [our] song,
Praising my [our] Savior all the day long."
(Fanny Crosby)

Chapter 2

The Joyful Blessings

"But thanks be to God! He gives us the victory through our Lord Jesus Christ." (1 Corinthians 15:57)

The following is just a glimpse of what we say in the short time that we may have to speak to the moms before they go into the abortion centers:

Please let me give you information before you go in. You haven't been told all the facts. There is a possibility of many complications. Read the consent form. I am telling you the truth. You are very special, don't hurt yourself. Your baby is a gift from God. Don't reject His gift. Choose life for your baby, please! – Sharon

Please think about what you are doing. Your baby is already formed inside of you. She is not a piece of tissue. Please look at this information and know what your reproductive rights are. You can keep your baby. We are here to help you. – Linda

If there is a part of you that says don't do it, then don't do it! You are special, please don't hurt yourself. Your baby is unique and has a plan and purpose in this life. No matter what it seems like, abortion is not the solution to the problem. You are not alone. We will help you. – Bonnie

Every sidewalk counselor in our area is trained in four areas: the complications that can and do occur because of the surgical procedure, fetal development from conception, what help is available and how to have a compassionate heart for the aborted woman.

The sidewalk counselors have pamphlets written in a simple and truthful manner, explaining the abortion procedures, some of the complications and the phone numbers and addresses of local crisis centers that will assist the mom in every way. We also have pamphlets to be given out after the abortion. These pamphlets let the women know that someone cares and if they are hurt in any way, emotionally, physically, or spiritually there are phone numbers to call for assistance and counseling. Within each pamphlet is a salvation tract. I always have used one with a rose on the front with the words, "You're Special." We want the women to know that they are special and we truly do care for them.

Most of the women going into an abortion center do not think much of themselves at that point in their lives. The "You're Special" tract shows them that they are special and it breaks down the walls that prevent communication.

Pro-life Christians endeavor to be at the abortion centers during all the hours when abortions are being committed. When blessed with enough people, they are also there when the moms come out. Many times they need rides home and it gives us the opportunity to minister love to them. Unfortunately that doesn't happen often anymore. There has been a serious decline of Christians willing to take a stand in the last few years.

Since 1988, when sidewalk counseling became a driving force in our community and across the country, there have been thousands of women who have walked away, drove away, and received the assistance offered instead of going through the abortion. Thanks be to our Lord!

This chapter includes just a few of the victories. Many, many times there have been "saves" that go unrecorded because our purpose is not to keep a count but to save lives and be a light for the love of Jesus.

However, we do have the following testimonies from Christian warriors across the nation. Written in their own words to give honor to our King. May you be blessed and encouraged in the reading of them:

In 1988, New York City. The day is bleak, rainy and chilly. As I sit on the stoop outside the police barracks my tears fall as quickly as the drops of rain from the sky. My heart is broke, my mind filled with contrition. My coat is drenched with water, I sob and sob.

That morning we 'rescued' and were arrested for saving life. I was released quickly, with only a minor charge. But a dear sister in the Lord was being detained and possibly facing serious charges that could cause her to lose her job. We both did the same thing but that's how the system works! I wept for the 'little ones' we all tried to save, I wept for my country that allows this atrocity to continue, I wept for the moms and I wept for my sister because of the cost she might pay. Suddenly there was a pro-lifer by my side. I looked up and she said, 'Come, get out of the rain, join us for coffee, it will be all right.' I arose and accompanied her to a nearby restaurant. Wet and cold, I removed my jacket.

That day I had on a tee shirt that had a pro-life message on it. As I sat at the counter the waitress approached me. She read my shirt and said, 'Can you help me? My friend is scheduled for an abortion tomorrow. I know it's wrong but I don't know what to do.'

We helped, the baby was saved and the woman in crisis received the assistance and love she needed. If I had not been on that stoop in the rain, if that pro-lifer had not felt sorry for me, if I had not been released early, if I had not put that shirt on that morning (I was the only one with a pro-life shirt on) that baby would be dead and that mother would be damaged for life. No matter how it seems; God is in control. By the way, the sister I was concerned about did not get a serious charge. Glory to the King! – Nancy

From Ken, a prayer warrior:

A young lady and her boyfriend were just about to enter the abortion center and the young man turned around and looked at us praying. He then grabbed his girlfriend's hand and they walked away from the center. We praised God for His mercy on this family!

Bill gives us two testimonies:

I am a sign bearer, the sign I hold is of an eight week, pre-born baby complete and right next to it is a picture of an aborted baby the same age. The contrast says it all. Recently we arrived at the abortion center before it opened and a car parked right behind ours. The young lady in the car looked at the sign, took our literature and left. We stayed at the center throughout all its abortion performing hours and this woman never returned!

Again we arrived before the center opened. A young lady parked near us. We had the opportunity to speak quietly with her. We gave her our information and showed her pictures of babies the same gestation as hers. She left and never returned. Thank You Jesus!

Dawn, a sidewalk counselor, shares this with us:

I was blessed with a 'save' in November. Angela was thirteen weeks pregnant. She went into the center and came back out crying. She realized that she could not go through with it. She had taken the information I offered and while inside, read it and saw what her unborn child looked like. Rashaan was born in June. I still keep in touch with her. I drove her to all her doctor appointments and we had a beautiful baby shower for her.

From Nancy:

It's Wednesday morning, I arrive at the center praying that the Lord would use me as a witness of His love and truth. As I was praying a car parked across the street. Immediately I approached the car and a young *woman along with her mother got out. 'May I give you information regarding abortions and your reproductive rights?' 'Get the #*#*#* away from us!' was the response. Yet, I continued speaking in a quiet voice, telling them about the complications, how the baby was growing and the help that is available. They were very angry and threatened to hit me but again I continued. Lives were in the balance, how could I explain to our heavenly Father that I stopped trying because of their anger or threats? They went in, I cried, I prayed and ten minutes later they came out. With the same hostile voices they said to me, 'Well here we are, now what?' Praise God, not only was the baby saved and the young lady's needs were met but both the mom and grandmother accepted Jesus one week later!*

"How great is his joy in the victories You give!" (Psalm 21:1b)

Karen shares this with us:

One Friday morning I arrived early, and the guard was already there. No one was coming in and I had the opportunity to witness to him about Jesus as Savior. After a few minutes of listening intently he accepted Christ as Savior! That day he quit being a guard for the center.

Taking a visible stand for the little ones has so many side benefits. The opportunities to witness to the unsaved, one on one are countless. I cannot count the amount of times we were privileged with the opportunities to help someone out. Most of the abortion centers are in poor neighborhoods. Many times homeless folks approach us for handouts. Instead of just giving them money, we take them to a Christian home. Instead of just appeasing our conscience with the token dollar, we make sure they are fed, clothed, given the salvation message and serious attempts are made to put them on the right track in life.

Sometimes it works and other times they just go right back into their old lifestyle. But, as with all ministry, we are called to be faithful, the rest is up to the Lord.

I remember one little boy in particular. Every Saturday morning when there would be a large number of pro-lifers at the center, this youngster would come and talk to us. Eventually, we became friends and we discovered that his life was very difficult. Living in a single parent home, not much food, clothing or love; this was one sad little boy. We took up a collection and bought him new winter clothes, we sent food home with him and of course gave him a Bible and led him to Jesus. I believe for a long time the pro-lifers kept in contact with this little boy.

Saturday morning before Mother's Day:

This is one of the most difficult days to go to an abortion center. It is almost too heart wrenching. To see the young women go in on this particular day is very emotionally draining. However, the Lord always meets us, comforts us and shows us a special victory. If we saw all the victories that have been won because we were there, we would start to take credit for them and that would not be a good thing.

Once again, our Lord gets all the glory and honor and we must never forget that. And on this Saturday morning Jesus had mercy and let us be part of a beautiful save.

A couple arrived at the center and I approached their car. 'Please take the time to read this information before you go. We are out here because we care.' The father said; 'We have a baby at home and just can't have another one right now.' I replied; 'But you already have another one, it will work out, when we do the right thing God truly blesses.'

The woman then said, 'I knew if someone was here we wouldn't be able to do it. Thanks for being here, we really don't need any help, I think we just needed someone to set us straight.' We hugged, and then they left." – Linda

A sidewalk counselor who had not seen a save for a long time wrote, "I rejoice in the saves by others, as I know the Lord blesses us all through each other. – Jackie

How true this is. Many times we have baby showers for the moms. Sometimes it turns out to be two or three moms at one time. Then we all join together and have a wonderful time. To see the moms happy and at peace with their little ones growing safely in their wombs is a joy like no other! What does it matter who did the talking at the abortion center, we are all the body of Christ. Our showers of love are not just for the moms but for us to rejoice with them.

Sometimes we don't know what God is accomplishing through us, as we see in the next testimony:

A Pastor was invited to speak at a college outside of New York City several years ago. His pro-life message was received into the heart of a young woman in the audience. She took the message home and shared it with her sister, who was scheduled for an abortion later that week. Her sister changed her mind and that baby is alive just because a Pastor spoke the truth to a group of college students.

Every once in a while we received such wonderful words of encouragement:

Hi, my name is George, I'm from Thailand. I'm attending the [University of Buffalo] to receive my P.H.D. in physics. I see you here week after week and no matter what the weather is like. I just wanted to stop and commend you on your faithfulness and tell you that you all are an inspiration to me. In Thailand, we do not kill our babies and I do not understand your country. It is good to see someone who cares.

The Lord always seems to send someone or something along to encourage us to keep on keeping on!

Now here's a wonderful Birthday present:

On August 1st, which is my birthday; two sisters in the Lord and I were standing outside an abortion center counseling and passing out pamphlets. Three women we had talked to before they went in, came out and had changed their minds! What a birthday present. – Pastor Darren

It's ok if the moms and dads get angry at us:

I gave a father our information and he went in to get his girlfriend out. She was very angry but that's ok because the baby is alive today. I also witnessed to them about Jesus and believe seeds were planted. – Tammy

Amber, did you ask Jesus?

While counseling near a driveway at a local abortion center, a car with an official seal on the door pulled up and parked on the street. I approached the car as two women were getting out. One woman was probably in her twenties and the other one was older. Not knowing which one was contemplating the abortion I said, 'Hi, if you know of anyone who had had an abortion or is thinking of having one would you please take this literature and share it with them?' Having said this, the older woman took the information and said, 'I have come here to have the abortion.' I asked if she would take a few minutes and talk before she made this life changing decision.

As we talked, she told me that she had a one year old baby at home and was shocked when she found out she was pregnant again. Because of her age she felt she just couldn't handle another baby. I asked her if she knew Jesus and she said yes. I then asked her if she had considered Him in her decision and she said no. After talking for quite a while she wanted to keep her baby and go home.

The younger woman with her was her daughter. She was very happy that her mom was not going to have the abortion. They both were very relieved and both wept openly.

Mable is a sweet lady. She told me she was on public assistance, went to a good church and believed between the church and assistance she didn't need any further help. However, she did take the numbers of our local agencies that offer much assistance.

We prayed, hugged and cried together. Then Mable, her daughter, and the "little one" safe inside went home. Praise to our Lord Jesus. Please say a prayer for Mable. – Bonnie

Dear Sarah Rose...
(It doesn't get much better than this!)

This miraculous event all began in August of '94 on a late Tuesday evening. It was the eve before my sidewalk counseling shift. We hadn't had a save in weeks and I was honest enough with myself to know I needed to get on my knees in prayer. After an hour of praying the Lord Jesus spoke to my heart in a particular way. He reminded me of His mother's "yes" to God. She had completely accepted His perfect will for her to become a mother. Mary, an unwed mother, trusted our Lord to do His will no matter how much persecution she might have to face. My prayer was that all unwed mothers could have the same courage and trust in God to say yes to Him and give life to their child.

I arrived at the abortion center at 7:20A.M. I parked in the metered spot across the street from the center. It was a bright, sunny Wednesday morning and I knew something marvelous was to occur that day. No sooner had I gotten out of my car when an old beat up car was pulling in right behind me.

In the car was a young couple with the woman on the passenger side. I approached her door as they began to get out and handed her pamphlets. She accepted it and got back into the car. I stood at a distance and watched as they read the material. The other counselors and I prayed the material would change their minds. Ten minutes went by very slowly as they remained in the car. Time, Jesus and the whole heavenly court was on our side. Then, as if in a hurry, they got out of the car and started walking towards the center. Another counselor and I approached them from behind. They stopped. I showed them my album (many counselors had albums with pictures of the developing baby, the accurate possible complications from the abortion procedure, those types of things). She explained that she thought she was pregnant because she was so sick to her stomach. She said she couldn't possibly have the baby because of her medical condition. I explained that if she was not in good health the last thing she should do was to have an abortion due to all the possible complications and side effects that can and do occur with an abortion.

This lady had no idea about the complications from the abortion procedure and became very concerned. I was able to walk them down the street as far as I could, away from the center. We stopped because she felt like vomiting. We then sat down on a stoop which happened to be in the alcove of a church.

Both of them proceed to tell me about their situation. They already had a daughter Rachael. We had exchanged names by now and Joseph showed me her picture. She was just beautiful. Joseph and Elizabeth felt that their families would be far too upset if they had another child. Money was tight, they weren't married and, most poignantly, Elizabeth's mother had just passed away. I asked Joseph how he felt about Elizabeth having their baby. He said he would stand beside her. Elizabeth was still clearly grieving the loss of her mother, who had been very important in her life, especially when she had her daughter, Rachael.

I told her she needed to see a good doctor as soon as possible. She lived outside the local area and disliked her current doctor. I gave her a pregnancy test to take home and administer herself. I said I would call her that afternoon about one o'clock with an appointment to see a reliable doctor. We walked back to the car, embraced and said good-bye. As they drove off, I broke into tears of joy. The miracle I had waited for had arrived and was orchestrated by the almighty hand of God!

When I returned to the abortion center to continue counseling the other moms going in, my partner informed me that the owner of the center was furious. The workers in the center were outside and proceeded to tell me that the security guard saw me walking away with the couple. Upon seeing this, the guard immediately beeped inside and informed the owner of what was going on. She quickly came out extremely upset that she had lost this opportunity for financial gain.

As soon as I arrived home I called my pro-life doctor and set up an appointment for Elizabeth for the following day. At the prescribed time I called with the good news. She already felt better; she just needed someone to lean on. I told her I would be with her every step of the way. This was to be the beginning of a beautiful and long lasting relationship.

After her appointment Elizabeth called me. She was pregnant, in good health and in no danger in this pregnancy. I offered to take her to the doctor appointments but Joseph took time off of work to take her.

As time went by I reassured her that all of the baby's material needs would be met. Her pregnancy was uneventful but, as usual, at the end very uncomfortable. Elizabeth had her moments of anxiety, unsure of what the future held for her and her children. Then we would talk of her mother, her life, her daughter and that would always help. Being able to express your emotions is always beneficial. Her mom was a devout Catholic and the mother of twelve children. She had prayed diligently for all of them and was there for Elizabeth in love and support throughout her first pregnancy. Once while driving Elizabeth for a blood test she admitted her mother would have been very upset that she had even thought about getting an abortion.

March finally rolled around and all of Elizabeth's and the baby's material needs had been met. Joseph and Elizabeth were ready. They had moved into a larger apartment and registered at a new parish. During the pregnancy both of them realized (thank You, Jesus) that "living together" was wrong and had agreed on a marriage in the fall.

Then the long awaited call came. It was Joseph. On March 6, 1995 Sarah Rose was born. Weighing in at 8lbs., 15oz. and 20" long, Sarah Rose was more beautiful then we all could have imagined.

I visited her at the hospital the next day. She was thrilled over the birth of her new baby daughter and was already anxious to go home. At times she seemed a little blue and I'm sure it was because of the absence of her mom. But joy overshadowed the sorrow and we praise the Lord for that. She confessed to me that she couldn't believe she had ever even though about having the abortion. We both cried and hugged each other. It was a very emotional moment.

I had the pleasure of visiting them at home. Sarah grew chubbier every time I saw her. Elizabeth registered Sarah for baptism at her church and I had the honor of being invited to attend the ceremony on Father's Day!

On that day I met each side of their families. I sat in the pew as the baby was christened, with tears of joy, a humble heart and in awe of our Lord Jesus' love and power. Here, on His holy altar, was the child who had escaped the horror of a painful death! She was now being baptized in His holy Name. It doesn't get any better than this I thought. "Thank you Lord, for Sarah. Bless her, Elizabeth, Rachael and Joseph all the days of their lives. – Dawn

That was just one of so many testimonies that are experienced by the Christians who put their feet to their belief. So many of the pro-life Christians follow through with love, friendship and assistance on their own as opposed to sending the mothers to crisis centers. All too often we hear or read about "those radical right wingers at the abortion centers." Too often we hear, "all they care about is the fetus and getting the woman to change her mind," and that is such a flagrant lie! We care about the mothers, the fathers, their needs, materials, emotions, and spiritual lives. Often those needs are met at a great personal sacrifice. The testimonies you are reading are not the exceptions, but indeed take place all the time!

The following testimony is what happens when no one but Jesus is watching:

But Look How Far She Came

During the "Summer of Mercy" in Wichita, Kansas, I was sidewalk counseling. One morning I knew the Lord wanted me to go to one particular abortion center. This one was not supposed to be open because of all the 'rescues' taking place that day. Yet, in obedience to the Lord's direction I went at 5:30 in the morning to the 'closed' abortion center. At about 6:00 A.M. a car with three young girls pulled into the empty lot. I got out of my car and started to approach theirs. They raced out of the lot and went up a one way street; the wrong way and were almost hit head on. As the morning progressed, more women came and I had the opportunity to talk one on one to them because all the police, pro-aborts and media were at the other abortion centers.

Later that morning, pro-lifers started coming and soon a mini 'rescue' was taking place. During the afternoon I partnered up with a woman who lived in this city (I am from western New York state). I was glad to have this wonderful woman with me because she knew where the local crisis-pregnancy centers were. In the meantime, all morning and afternoon I had observed the three girls seen early that morning, constantly circling the abortion center, but never stopping.

Every time I would try to talk to them (about five times) they would speed away. Finally, about 3:30 that afternoon I saw them go past the center and park about one block away. I waited until they got out of the car and were about a half of a block from the center. Then my partner and I walked to them. They actually stopped to listen to us.

We found out that they were 'Christian' girls; two of them had come for support for the third girl. Her mom did not know she was pregnant, neither did the father of the baby. She was to enter college in the fall and was so ashamed she was pregnant and had been sexually active that she thought abortion was the only answer.

After talking for about twenty minutes she did agree to go to the local crisis-pregnancy center with us. They said they would follow us in their car. The C.P.C. was some distance from the abortion center so we were concerned that they would turn their car around and go back to the abortion center. Needless to say, much prayer was going up to our Lord as we went to the store front C.P.C.! We arrived there at 5:00 and the center was closed. Therefore, we quickly went to plan B and took the girls to dinner to buy some time. My partner called a person who worked in the C.P.C. and she said she would be there in about one hour. Perfect! Just the right amount of time to have a nice dinner and more time to talk to the ladies.

We found a Chinese restaurant, sat down and ordered our meal. It was at this time I realized that I didn't have any money with me! I whispered to my partner: 'I don't have any money, do you?' Her answer was, "No!"

Plan C. I excused myself, canceled my order and left to go back to the abortion center to see if there was still any pro-lifers there that I could borrow money from. I now had to find my way back to the center on my own. It was only by God's mercy that I was able to do this. After driving through an intense rain storm I arrived at the center. A few people were still there and with humility I asked them to lend me money and explained the purpose for the need. Without hesitation the pro-lifers gave me what they could spare.

Finding my way back to the restaurant was a little easier. As I arrived they were just finishing their meal and they never did know how close we all were to washing dishes that night! Jesus is so good; the money the people donated covered the bill and the tip almost to the penny.

We talked a little more and the 'mom' by now had completely changed her mind. I asked them why they kept driving away whenever I tried to approach the car. They said they were afraid of me. I asked them why? I hadn't run up to them or shouted or did anything except walk toward them. They told us they had come to the city the night before and stayed in a local motel. They heard on the news that Operation Rescue was in town for the

Summer of Mercy. The newscasters had painted us in an extremely negative way. When they saw me they thought I might damage the car they were in. How very sad.

I then asked them why they ended up stopping to talk to us. The "mom" said; "When I heard you say, 'If there is one little part of you that says don't do it, then please don't.' She said, 'That really touched my heart.'

Thanks be to God, there was the part of her, the conscience that God puts in us, to know right from wrong and she chose the right! Interestingly, as they were following us to the C.P.C., the mom said to her friends, 'Maybe we should just go back to the abortion center. After all, we drove five hours to get here.' One of her friends replied, 'Yes, but look how far she came to tell you not to go in.

The mom and her friends went back home, happy yet with many things to do. She had to tell her parents, her boyfriend and be ready to face all her friends and relatives. With the help of our Lord she did do it all and was truly blessed. This young lady married her boyfriend, started college in the fall as planned and is now the mother of a wonderful baby boy!

The counselor from Wichita was a great help to her. They still keep in contact and I have been blessed to see a picture of the little boy. All thanks, praise and honor to our Lord Jesus Christ! – Bonnie

What an incredible true story. Just a few things to think about: Bonnie was at the abortion center at 5:30, which means she had to be out of bed around 4:00. She never left her post until 3:30 that afternoon. That's ten and half hours of diligent, prayerful, sustained activity in her efforts to offer help to the women going in. Bonnie never did eat dinner and probably didn't eat lunch either. Did what Bonnie went through to save the life of that little boy and help that mom ever make the news? No, it did not. But let me tell you, it sure made headlines in the heavenly realm and that's where it matters.

A sister in the Lord sent me this next testimony. I could not make out her name but her rewards are in heaven anyway. May you be as touched by this as I was:

Christmas of '94 was perhaps the closest to the spirit of the season as I have ever experienced. To fully appreciate all the Lord has done, you have to understand that I am truly the least of His servants. No false modesty, just painfully true. The strength, fire, courage and selflessness I so admire in many of my brothers and sisters in the Lord, I lamentably lack in myself. Timid, quiet and shy are more appropriate characterizations. Mine is not the clabber of clay the Master would select to mold into a vessel suitable for His use.

However, the love, grace and mercy of our Lord is beyond comprehension, beyond preconceived assumption and beyond description. He not only moves in mysterious ways, but His ways surprise us... fills us with joy and wonder that we cannot imagine or anticipate. He does, indeed, choose the foolish things of the world and lifts up the lowly.

Having spent a week's vacation in the "Spring of Life" in 1992, which was a major rescue activity in Buffalo, New York, my pro-life view was rather well know in the office I work in. A co-worker, Christy, who is a dear friend in the Lord and knew of my experience, took me aside and asked if I would speak to her niece. Christy's brother and sister-in-law, godly parents, and their daughter Betsy were in a very volatile situation. Betsy had become a rebellious teenager and was now pregnant. Adding to the dilemma, the father of the unborn child was a married man. Having gone through months of stormy times, the family was at a dangerous point. Christy told me that Betsy was not going to abort her baby; however, whether that decision would remain steadfast was dubious. Further, she hoped I might facilitate reconciliation in the family.

Arrangements were made and I met with Betsy. We met in a small neighborhood restaurant. I prayed a great deal for guidance, for wisdom and for His will to be complete in all that transpired. Nonetheless, I remained apprehensive. Assuming I was there to share the love of

Jesus in hope of reconciliation with her family, I did not focus on abortion.

However, the Lord gave me presence of mind to take my pro-life album with me. Most of the sidewalk counselors at that time carried these albums and they were an effective tool in sharing with a woman in a crisis pregnancy. My album contained pictures of fetal development, pictures of aborted babies, lists of complications, consent forms from local abortion providers and lists of help available.

To continue, not only did Betsy show up, she brought her sister to our meeting. Betsy appeared withdrawn and was unwilling to communicate. However when I opened my album and started to share about the development of her baby, Betsy became very interested. When we came to the stage of development that her baby was now in, she even asked if she could hold the album and look at it herself. After a few minutes Betsy started to open up and communicate. She shared how bleak she felt her future to be. I proposed talking with her parents and if negotiations failed I would make arrangements for her to stay with my Pastor and his family. This family had taken in other young women in similar situations.

Betsy did stay with this family for a little while. But that didn't work out either. It seems when a teen is in rebellion they are totally unwilling to have any perimeters set. From that point until the arrival of her little baby girl in December, Betsy drifted between a part time apartment with the father of the baby and her parents home

News of Betsy became very sporadic. She left the married man, the family reconciled, she met a nice man and they were married. One year later Christy confided in me that Betsy and her husband were struggling financially. She then asked if I could help her purchase gifts for Christmas and the baby's first birthday. I was happy to do so and had a great time shopping for the presents. Christy then took all we had bought over to Betsy's home.

Christy came back to work after giving the gifts and presented me with a beautiful picture of Betsy's daughter. She had tears in her eyes and in a voice barely above a whisper Christy said, "Betsy had lied, she did intend on having an abortion." At this point we're now both crying. She continued, "Guess what the Lord used to change her mind, melt her heart? The pictures in your album! Her daughter's name is Cassie." I wanted to yell her name out to one and all. Cassie, a beautiful precious life. She lives by the grace and mercy of the Lord Jesus Christ!

This was more than I could have hoped for. Yet the Lord was not finished. The revelations were to continue. More miracles coming up! A few days later Christy was on the phone telling me that Betsy would like to speak to me, to thank me for the gifts I had given them. We exchanged pleasantries and the thank yous. Then she divulged that she had a lot of explaining to do to her husband. He had known, obviously, about Cassie and Betsy's circumstances but never had told him about our meeting. So when Christy brought the gifts over, Betsy's husband was curious as to who I was. She then she told him, "This was the woman who turned my life around. I was going to abort Cassis but because of her I didn't and we now have our beautiful daughter. It was the best decision I've ever made. My life was a terrible mess and I got it straight. She changed my life.

I am so truly honored that the Lord used me and I really wept for joy!

The redemptive power of our Lord and His continual diverse applications of it; one touch by the Master and lives are transformed. Transformed in ways we could never anticipate; rippling into and touching other lives as He guides the current. I'm still an inadequate grade of clay, but oh what a mighty grateful one! Amazing grace has taken on a far deeper significance. Not only did He save a wretch like me, He actually chose to use me to save the lives of others. Praise the name of Jesus." – One Mighty Warrior

The testimony you just read is one of many instances where the pro-lifer used their training in situations other than in front of an abortion center. When we know what we are talking about and have had experience on the "front lines" the Lord uses us wherever we are.

As for me; one time I was at a department store standing at a counter waiting for an item. There was no indication that I was a Christian pro-lifer, such as a button or shirt. Yet, the woman next to me started to talk about abortion. I had the opportunity to communicate the truth to her. It was a wonderful experience. We surely serve an awesome God!

In my experiences I have observed that when you take a visible stand for Jesus on the mission field, especially a tough one, the Lord gives you His eyes to see, His ears to hear and His heart to feel. The more we serve Him in a visible and active way the more He gives us to do for Him. The awareness of what is going on around us becomes finely honed. The boldness to witness of His love and life-giving message becomes strong and true.

The following is a statement from a bold sidewalk counselor regarding what she has learned by being active in the battle against abortion. I believe what is said here speaks for many of us:

I have learned not to operate in guilt but indeed in love. When I first became a sidewalk counselor, I used to become very frustrated and the negative emotions were very predominant. However, the Lord is constantly helping me, by His Holy Spirit, to produce love, kindness, gentleness, goodness, joy, peace, patience, faithfulness and self-control. And I trust that He will continue to help me grow in all those areas. I truly believe that God is letting the mothers make their choice just as He does with salvation. I thank Him for all the Christians that bring the opportunity to make the right choice to the pregnant women in crisis." – Terry

Becoming a part of this difficult ministry makes one grow up in the Lord rather quickly. In order to continue going to the local abortion centers, one must mature in Christ or he/she will definitely end up quitting.

In our area we have a team of sisters (we always go to the centers in teams, never alone) who sidewalk counsel once a week for two hours and once a month on Saturdays. They have been doing this for quite a few years and are strong Christian women. Here is what they say about being out there:

As for my sister and I, we will never give up, no matter how hopeless it looks. We'll keep on trying. I thank God that He woke us up but more that that, He got us involved. We are also determined not to get burned out. At the end of our shift, we pray and leave the heartbreak at the foot of the Cross. We then leave the center immediately unless the Lord impresses on us to stay longer. The most important part of our being out there is to win souls for Christ. Nothing will really change until hearts are changed. We need to be at the abortion centers to give the message of hope in Jesus. We also need to let the moms know they'll have to answer to God someday, unless they repent. And because we have told them the truth, they are without excuse." – Jackie

Here's a testimony from these sisters about a save they experienced:

My sister and I had a save recently. There was a young couple that crossed the street and headed down the driveway to the entrance of the abortion center. I spoke to them and the woman kept pulling away from the man as they were walking. I just knew the Lord was going to do something. He prompted me to turn around shortly after they went behind the wall (this abortion center entrance was behind a very large wall). It was then that I saw the woman leaning against the building at the end of the driveway, crying. When I saw her crying I asked my sister to start praying hard because I knew the Lord was moving.

I spoke some words of love and encouragement in hopes that she would choose life for her unborn child. A few minutes later they came up the driveway smiling! The woman said to me, 'Don't worry the baby is still inside me.' My sister gave them our pro-life information and they left knowing that they had made the right decision. – Jackie & Linda

Thus far all of the testimonies you have read have been victories because we allowed Jesus to work in us and motivate us. He calls and we are obedient. However, the following testimony is a miracle because it never could have happened in the natural. Let me set the scenario up for you:

Every Saturday morning the *clinic defenders* used to be out in full force. They were obnoxious, rude, and violent and would do anything they could which included using whistles, squirt guns, shouting, pushing, hitting, and surrounding a woman going in so we would not have opportunity to offer any type of information to them. It used to be very difficult to offer the moms-in-crisis any choice, love or knowledge of help that was available to them. The spiritual battle was very intense and everyone was very charged up.

This one particular Saturday I was at one of the local abortion centers. The driveway sloped down into a fenced in parking lot. The women would walk down this driveway and be out of sight very quickly. The place is now closed and we praise the Lord for that. Yet, on this morning it was very busy and there were about fifteen defenders. They were standing on each side of the driveway to prevent us from offering the moms any information...

We all were in intense prayer as it seemed hopeless for any opportunity to speak to the moms.

We knew it had to be His sovereign move that would save the life of a baby and touch the heart of a mom. As we were praying a young woman was spotted walking down the street. I approached her with the pamphlet in hand and started to speak gently to her. The defenders usually run, and I mean run, up to whoever we are talking to, push us aside, rip the literature from their hands and surround her until she in inside and the baby's death is sealed.

However, today God had mercy and in His mercy not one defender moved from the driveway. This young lady was listening but would not stop walking. I just walked with her, not wanting to give up. We approached the driveway, lined up with the pro-aborts. The young mom stopped in the middle of the driveway. No one moved! It was like all of them were in a daze. We, the young lady and I, stood there and quietly spoke for several minutes. She changed her mind about getting the abortion and we walked away in peace. I took her home and all is well with her and her child. A miracle had taken place, God supernaturally intervened; **"You prepare a table before me in the presence of my enemies." (Psalm 23:5a)** Don't ever doubt the living God!

The Lord works in His own ways:

There was an abortionist in our town that we have been praying for since 1987. As a matter of fact, there have been many times that we have personally witnessed to this man in love. We bought him a beautiful Bible for Christmas one year and continually beseeched the Lord to have this "doctor" stop killing children. One year ago he was caught committing an abortion on a child that was past the age of viability in a hospital where that is not allowed. He lost his medical license. I believe that our Lord answered our prayers in His way. This abortionist lost everything and perhaps now he will turn his life over to Jesus. And the whole thing was orchestrated by the Lord in such a way that only He can receive all the glory!

In recent years so many abortionists have been either exposed, denied their license or have chosen to stop on their own. The Lord in His mercy is answering our prayers and rewarding the steadfastness of His saints. Being faithful and not giving up is essential to victory.

Read how being tenacious truly pays off:

There was a guard at one of the local abortion centers that I continually prayed for. He really was a nice man, unsaved and not really understanding what an abomination abortion is. Every time I counseled when he was working I would talk to him and witness the love of Jesus. This continued for over a year.

Eventually he started to tell me about the women who changed their minds but didn't come out until after all the pro-lifers left. That was awesome because there were a lot of them. However, because of the evil influence from his employer, this guard became angry and withdrawn. Then I was arrested on false charges and this guard went to court and lied on the stand against me. I was sent to prison for a period of time. Upon my release I immediately went back to this abortion center to resume my duties as a sidewalk counselor. When the guard saw me he became very upset. I approached him with a smile and told him, "I have never stopped praying for you. I'm not angry with you. I just want you to meet Jesus and get your life straight." He was so touched that he started to cry and that was the beginning of this man coming to Jesus!

Now at the same time the Lord had put the director of this abortion center on my heart. Every time she would come out of the center to either see what was happening or to go to the post office (just across the street) I would talk to her and confront her with the truth of what she was doing. At this time I had a little cassette player and a tape of a ten week pre-born baby's heartbeat. Every time I had the opportunity to talk to her I also played the heartbeat. This went on for quite some time without ever getting a response from her. Then one day when no one else was around she stopped and talked to me. It was a positive conversation and I invited her to have lunch together. Shock of shocks, she said yes!

Let me pause here to say that I surely wasn't the only one praying for this woman and the guard. A pastor who was faithfully with us on the street also was interceding for those two. Also, during this time we had found out that the director and the guard had been dating. Therefore, we decided to invite the both of them to lunch and God made it work.

Praise His holy name the luncheon was a complete success. We have discovered that when we can get someone away from the centers they really listen to the truth. It truly is a marvel! That luncheon was the beginning of a special relationship. At Christmas time Pastor Darren and I bought our two special friends gifts and our prayers continued to go before the Lord. Then it happened; both of them accepted Jesus Christ as their Savior and both of them quit working at the abortion center. We attended their wedding and it was great! We kept in contact for a long time and they have given their testimony on several occasions at pubic functions.

After losing contact with them, I have recently found out that they both are still strong Christians and are serving the Lord!

It took years of loving, not judging these two precious children of God and I will always be thankful that the Word of God states, **"Let us not become weary in doing good, for at the proper time we will reap a harvest if we do not give up." (Galatians 6:9)** Our Lord never promised us easy or fast. He said be steadfast and faithful.

The following is a word of encouragement from a faithful sign bearer:

I'm encouraged: When I see moms leaving with their baby still within. When Christians stay that extra hour and don't leave after their two hour shift because the moms keep going in. I'm encouraged when I hear others preaching from the Bible. I've been honored many times to witness wonderful 'saves'. I've seen women turn their cars around and not come back because we were there. I've seen counselors walking off with the 'moms' to the nearby restaurants and coming back excited because the mom changed her mind. I've seen dad's speaking to the counselors and then going into the center and bringing their wife or girlfriend out. Friends have brought friends out because we were there. I've seen our pamphlets left on windshields used in a powerful way. I'm truly blessed by being with the brethren in this battle for life. I have the privilege of holding a sign that effectively works to change a mom's mind and choose life for their baby. –Allen

Seeing a mother choose life for her child is an awesome experience. However, there are long periods of time when we do not *see* any victory. Steadfast in our commitment, we have been faithful in our going. We have been faithful in our counseling, praying, and holding signs; yet, many times we do not see any good coming out of it all. We know of Christians who show up, pray up and have never witnessed a save first hand.

Here's how they feel:

I have never been part of turning a woman away from an abortion center that I know of. In over three and half years I have never had that blessing. Discouraging? Yes! Disheartening? Yes! Many times I've distrusted my usefulness and effectiveness, yet I will continue to persevere. I can serve and save in many other ways. I believe it was Henry Hyde who said, 'It's not how many lives you save but did you try?' I've been able to teach Jr. High and High school students about abortion. I know I've made an impact on them. I pray they will remember my words and those of our heavenly Father.

Perhaps by my words one teenager will not get pregnant or will not go to an abortion center. The Lord has opened doors for me to speak about abortion in several churches. I know that some Christians have taken a visible stand because of my presentations. If all I can do is spread the Word and speak truth, then that is what I'll do. I'll know in eternity and that's all that matters. I rejoice in the 'saves' of others as the Lord blesses us all as His Body. – Eileen

"Now faith is being sure of what we hope for and certain of what we do not see." (Hebrews 11:1)

We hope, we pray, we believe and then:

I saw a young girl go in the front entrance of the center. There was no one guarding the entrance at this time. Therefore, I had the opportunity to go right up to the door with this young lady. I continued to talk to her even after she went inside because I knew she could hear me. I had just started to walk away and I heard the door open. I turned around and it was the young lady. She was from Pennsylvania (they came to N.Y.S. because they do not need parental permission here), she was sixteen years old. I asked her if she had come out because of what I said. She said, "Yes"! It was my first save and I cried with happiness a lot that day. Every time I told someone I would cry. Thank You, Jesus – Glory Ann

There is one particular abortion center in our area where we rarely see a woman change her mind, yet one day:

My partner and I had prayed, praised the Lord and read Scripture throughout our shift. I had come to the center prayed up and prepared to counsel as best as I could. No one had taken our information before going in and now it was time for some of the women to be finished and coming out. I then prepared to pass out the post-abortion pamphlets to these women. As I attempted to give a couple this information the man rolled down the window on his side of the car. He said, "No, we didn't do it!" My partner gave the couple information on where to go to get any help needed. They left with a smile on their face. Our Lord touched their hearts and we rejoice in His victory! – Sharon

Sometimes, when we can afford it, we buy pregnancy tests to pass out along with our pamphlets. It is always our hope the women will take it and not go in. In the packet we hand out is pro-life information, a salvation tract and the test. See, if the woman is just going in for a pregnancy test, they (the abortion center workers) do all they can to sell the lady an abortion. Therefore, the tests we give can be very effective in saving life.

The following is a pregnancy test turn away:

Our shift was over and we were just about ready to leave but for some reason we were still standing there. We noticed a young girl walking down the street and we began a conversation with her. We found out that she was going into the center for a pregnancy test. We offered her one free of charge and told her about the help that is available. Darla started to cry. She said that she was really touched that someone really cared. This young lady already had one child at home, was not married to the father and was on public assistance. With a thank you on her lips she took the pregnancy test and information and was relieved to know that help was available and she didn't have to be alone in her crisis. I am so glad we stayed that extra few minutes. – Debra

It is extremely interesting that in the pro-life ministry not one particular thing works more than another. Sometimes it is seeing the people praying, sometimes it's the words we say, sometimes it is the pamphlets we hand out, sometimes the signs do it and sometimes it is just because we are there. I have been told many stories about women who drove by and saw us there with signs and when the unplanned pregnancy happened they chose life for their child because of what they had seen. I have even heard testimonies of people coming back to the Lord because of our faithfulness. The bottom line here is it is the Holy Spirit who convicts of life and truth. We are just His vessels willing to be used in His Love.

Just telling someone that the Lord loves them can touch their heart:

One woman came to the abortion center in a taxi cab. I called out to her and told her, "God loves you. He forgives and gives strength to do the right thing." She still went in and while she lay on the table getting ready for the abortion she heard my words lingering in her mind. She jumped off the table and came out of the center. Her name is Denise. We prayed together and my partner drove her home with her little one safe and growing. – Eva

The Lord promised us in His Word:

"I will turn their mourning into gladness; I will give them comfort and joy instead of sorrow." (Jeremiah 31:13b)

"He answered their prayers because they trusted in Him." (1 Chronicles 5:20)

As we go our trust grows!

Susan writes:

When I arrived at the abortion center on Wednesday morning it was a real time of mourning. Before I got out of the car, three women went down the driveway into the center. No time, no opportunity to speak truth to them. My heart broke and all I could do was pray and ask God's forgiveness for not being there earlier.

Quickly, I put up our signs and prepared to intervene as best as I could. Our Lord is truly gracious and kind because He took that time of mourning and feeling of inadequacy and turned it into joy and praise. One hour after I had arrived, a couple stopped, listened to me and chose life for their child. All we need to do is be there. We need to be the voice of the innocent baby, we need to witness God's love and mercy to others and we need to let others know of the help that is available. It truly works!

When sidewalk counselors are trained the importance of prayer is stressed. To truly be effective we need to have clean hands and pure hearts. We need to let the Lord search us for anything that we need forgiveness for. Putting on our armor (Ephesians 6:10-18) is extremely important. Hearts need to be filled with His love in order to give it away. And our attitude must be one of humility. When we go to the abortion centers in this manner we are truly effective.

Debra, a sidewalk counselor, shares how she prepares her heart for the battle for life:

"I pray this Scripture for the sidewalk counselors and my partners: **'May the God who gives endurance and encouragement give you a spirit of unity among yourselves as you follow Christ Jesus, so that with one heart and mouth you may glorify the God and Father of our Lord Jesus Christ. Accept one another, then, just as Christ accepted you, in order to bring praise to God.' (Romans 15:5-7)**

When I go on the street I pray differently than I usually do. I have a forty-five minute drive and that's the time I take to pray. First, I thank God for the opportunity to serve Him and others. Then, I humble myself, knowing that I cannot be effective without Him. I ask Him to fill me with His Holy Spirit to overflowing so that others can see His love through me. I ask for mercy to be upon me, the moms, dads and even the abortionists. Then I bind the rulers, authorities, powers, the strongman and spiritual forces of evil in the heavenly realm. I pray that The Lord will release His Holy Spirit to fill the abortion center, the sidewalk, the street and the parking lot. I ask the Lord to go before me and fill the sidewalk with His glory. In doing this I receive a peace in knowing that the Lord will be with me and has heard my heart. Then I do my best to save the little ones and touch the hearts of the moms."

Pro-lifers are determined to never give up because we know that the next thing we say or do could be what will change the mind and heart of the women carrying their children into the abortion centers for termination.

Jerry and Dan share this with us:

It was a Thursday, September 28, 1995. I was going about my regular daily picket at the local hospital where they have an abortion center. About 9:25 A.M., Dan came around the corner with a sign from the trunk of my car. 'A BABY IS A PERSON NO MATTER HOW SMALL.' We both saw the young couple duck behind the fence and go down the sidewalk where Dan had just walked. They had stopped to finish smoking before going in. We then approached them and gave them the information regarding the facts and help that is available. The young man immediately threw it back at us, saying to us, 'We don't need your stuff, our minds are made up!' However, the young lady did seem interested; therefore, I tried to give our literature to her again. Again, the man took it from her and threw it back at us, now stepping in front of her to block us from seeing her.

We remained calm, retrieved the packet and continued to talk gently. We said, "You can come back next week if you don't go in today, but if you go in now you can't change your mind tomorrow." She replied, "I can't, I am already eleven weeks along."

Again we spoke, 'Many women are injured by abortion. We'll help you get your money back. You're the parents now, abortion will not change that. Don't you think that your mom and dad have a right to know? This baby is their grandchild. At least give them a chance to help. Please read this information and discuss it. This is a very important decision. Don't rush into this, you will regret it for the rest of your life.'

Then we walked down the sidewalk about one hundred feet to give them space to talk and give us the opportunity to pray. After five or six minutes, we knew we just couldn't leave it like it was. We went back for one more try. I offered to go with them just down the street to our Crisis Pregnancy Center. Praise the Lord they said; 'Alright!'. I gave Dan my sign and walked with them the two blocks to changed lives!

A familiar face greeted us in the office. Shelia is on my personal support and prayer list. I introduced her to Ray and Brandy and explained the situation to her. Shelia took them back to the counseling room and I went back to my post.

Dan and I continued to pray and hold our signs for another half an hour, afraid to leave. We praised the Lord because at the least they missed their appointment for that day. A short while later we received word that this young couple changed their minds and were going to let their baby live! They even went back to the abortion center on their own and got their money back!

The best is yet to be told:

Ten days later, on October 8th, Ray and Brandy accepted an invitation to a Christian Crusade. They both went forward to the altar and accepted Jesus Christ into their lives!

Perseverance works! Prayer does move mountains and faithfulness gets blessed.

It's not always about the women and babies. Often when pro-lifers are in front of the abortion centers, people drive by us and give us the finger, try to run us over, swear at us and are generally very cruel. Anger truly prevails in our country and anger comes from guilt. However, occasionally something very special happens, like the following testimonies:

One Wednesday morning I was at the local abortion center praying. It was my normal shift. I had been doing this for over one year. About one hour after I had been there a young man approached me. With a friendly smile, I struck up a conversation with him. He shared with me that every Wednesday he drove by and saw me here. No matter what the weather was I was here. He then told me that he had finally worked up the courage to stop and speak to me. He was desperate for help. He was a homosexual who wanted out from his sinful life but did not know how to change. I shared the Gospel with him and told him about a local organization that had been founded by men who had come out of this life style. He gave me his name and phone number and I told him I would get the number of this organization and call him. I did so the next day. He received the help he needed and now is a born again Christian. Thank you, Lord, for letting me be there when this man needed You! – Terry

Kathy shares the next two testimonies with us:

A male pedestrian about thirty to thirty-five years old walked toward Harry, Lou and I as we stood praying on Main Street, in front of Planned Parenthood. He took the packet of information that we pass out there. Then he began to openly discuss some of his personal problems. He shared his strong desire to experience a deeper sense of joy in his faith and how he wanted more power to live in the Spirit. After conversing with him for about twenty minutes, David accepted our offer to pray for him and lay hands on him. Immediately, God began to touch him! How incredibly beautiful it was to witness this man as he raised his hands to heaven in worship to the Lord. The Holy Spirit was truly filling him. A little time later, David asked us to go to his home and speak with his wife. Evidently they were having problems and David knew Jesus could solve them. In love, we went to his home and his wife received us, listened to us and finally prayed with us. It was our feeling that the Lord had really worked many blessings into David's family that day. Thank You, Jesus, for using us.

And...

On January 9th, we had the opportunity to have a heart to heart talk with a man after he walked out of Planned Parenthood. Eddy made a pledge of chastity right there on the street. He promised to uphold his pledge from this time on and recommitted his life back to Christ. With tears in his eyes he told us. 'Thank you for being faithful.'

Many times our own personal testimonies touch the heart of the lost. They see that they are not alone in their troubles and that Christians aren't perfect, just forgiven. Everyone has troubles and problems; the difference is how we handle them. As Christians we take our troubles and problems to the Cross and our Lord shows us how to handle them and then He gives us the strength to do so.

Sharon, who is normally a sign bearer, shares the following testimony of how we should never be afraid to share our own hurts and how God blesses us through them:

It certainly was a beautiful day!

The weather was beautiful on this Friday. I arrived at the clinic with counseling material. I am a sign bearer and prayer warrior but I always have information with me just in case. There was a lot of action that Friday and many pro-lifers were at the clinic.

A car pulled into the gas station that is right next to the clinic. I tried to signal the sidewalk counselor but she was already busy with someone. I approached the woman getting out of the car and asked her if she was pregnant and going into the clinic. She said, "No, I'm taking my daughter in." I talked to both the mother and daughter at great length. The older woman shared that her daughter was only fifteen and too young to have a baby.

I told her that I could understand how she feels as I also had a daughter who, at fifteen, became pregnant. I shared that pregnancy is natural and not at all as dangerous as abortion. Explaining the complications from abortion and all the help that was available, I sensed that the pro-lifers were praying for us as we conversed.

The older woman seemed very tense yet she did look straight into my eyes as I said, 'My granddaughter is the joy of my life and everything has worked out.' However, they still turned away and walked into the clinic. How hard it is to share your heart and they still walk in! Yet we continued to cry out to the Lord for mercy on this child, the mother and grandmother.

Well, praise the Lord, they came right back out! The grandmother seemed very relieved, like a great burden was lifted off her. We hugged and it was wonderful. They stood and talked with us all for a while. Taking all the information on help that is available they got in their car and waved with smiles on their faces as they drove off. It certainly was a wonderful day!

Sometimes we have the opportunity to participate in the birth process as a "coach" for a mom who had changed her mind and decided to have the baby. It is one of the biggest blessings a pro-lifer receives. Being *there* humbles us and re-enforces the truth about the sanctity of life.

My phone rang, "Nancy, I think I'm in labor. My pains are ten minutes apart. Can you come over and take me to the hospital?"

This was a mother who chose life instead of death for her little one when she was eight weeks pregnant. Together, she and I walked through her pregnancy. It was not easy; it never is. An unwanted pregnancy is a most difficult, emotional and confusing time in the life of a woman. Yes, we know that children are a gift from the Lord, but sometimes that truth takes time to become a reality in the heart.

When a young, single woman becomes pregnant unexpectedly, a million emotions begin to crash within her. We all know right from wrong, the Bible is very clear on that:

> *"When outsiders who have never heard of God's law follow it more or less by instinct, they confirm its truth by their obedience. They show that God's law is not something alien, imposed on us from without, but woven into the very fabric of our creation. There is something deep within them that echoes God's yes and no, right and wrong." (Romans 2:14, MSG)*

However, knowing sometimes doesn't help in a crisis, especially when we are young and alone. When something as unexpected and unwanted as pregnancy occurs, confusion can really overtake any sound decision making.

Questions fill the mind: why did I have sex in the first place? Why didn't I use birth control? What am I going to do now? How will my life ever be what I thought it would now? I don't want this baby. How can I tell my family? Why did this happen to me?

On and on the questions go and very rarely in the midst of the crisis does a young woman hear the correct answers.

Anguish fills the soul; "I know that having sex outside of marriage is wrong. I don't even love the father. God can never forgive me for this. Why did He allow this to happen to me?"

Physically, the body is rapidly changing. Hormones are bouncing all over the place, a new life within is growing rapidly. It is complicated, it is confusing and it is terrifying!

No woman is prepared for an unwanted pregnancy. And we, as ambassadors for Christ, must realize this. We endeavor, with all our hearts, to be compassionate and understanding when our Lord gives us the opportunity to work with one of these young mothers.

Sarah and I grew close during this difficult time. As the child grew within her, so did her love for the Lord, her child and herself. With a smile, a word of encouragement, a promise to be there, a touch, and loving without condemnation, the guilt, the anger, the confusion, and the self-condemnation vanished like fog on a sunny morning.

The pro-lifers had a baby shower for her. It was just wonderful and the baby's needs were met. Sarah and I went to Lamaze classes together and it was fun. Now it was time for her baby to be born.

"Relax (as I rubbed her legs), let your body do the work. Not much longer now. You're doing great!" Transition began and the doctor entered the room.

He broke her water sac and observed that the fluid was soiled. The baby had a bowl movement in the amniotic fluid while the sac was intact.

"It is imperative that the baby come quickly now." The doctor told us. He took me aside and said, "If the baby swallowed or breathed any of the soiled fluid, serious complications could occur such as retardation."

"Push, Sarah, push, you're almost done...." And her beautiful little daughter was born.

Quickly, the nurses took the little girl child and suctioned out her stomach and lungs. Everything looked great so far. As Sarah was delivering the placenta and receiving a few stitches, I kissed her and told her what a wonder she is. The baby had to go immediately into a special incubator because of the soiled fluid. She needed to be closely monitored for a short time.

The nurses allowed me to go with the little one and I was given the opportunity to put my hands through a special opening in the incubator. As I caressed her little frame, I prayed that the Lord would keep her perfect in Him. That was a truly love-filled moment for me.

Amber is fine and growing into a beautiful little girl. Sarah is struggling and in rebellion, still not fully committed to Christ; her life is full of confusion. But I pray for her and I know seeds of love and truth that were planted in her heart will someday grow. As with all things, the choice of paths to take is hers. She chose the right path in allowing her daughter to live, may she choose the path of Christ and live eternally with Him.

Being part of the birthing process has been a humbling and amazing experience. In participating as a coach in child birth I realized that we don't have to agree on everything to be a part of each other. In that indivisible piece of time, a complete oneness and selflessness is achieved. We become all-giving, all-hoping, and all-focusing on the birth of a little human being. As swift as a sunbeam, quick as a twinkle, life travels to life. From the moment of conception life is in existence. All that is needed from that moment on is time and nutrition. Forty-two weeks later that life from within is brought forth. To be a part of that moment is awesome indeed!

I have been honored to be a coach in nine births. Each time the moment is so overwhelming and miraculous; it is always like the first time.

How unique, how precious, what a purpose each of us have in this life. What a tragedy, what a travesty, what a grievous act abortion is! The Holy Word tells us:

> *I praise You because I am fearfully and wonderfully made; Your works are wonderful, I know that full well. My frame was not hidden from You when I was made in the secret place. When I was woven together in the depths of the earth, Your eyes saw my unformed body. All the days ordained for me were written in Your book before one of them came to be. (Psalm 139:14-16)*

Life – what a precious gift!

I have shared with you the wonderful victories of children saved, hearts touched, mothers and fathers loved into the Kingdom of the Lord. May your heart join ours as we sing for joy in the sweetness of life.

May we all grow deeper in our awareness of the plan and purposes each of us have in this life.

Now, I write of the heartbreak. For every save there are so many deaths. For every smile of joy there are a million tears that fall. For every salvation there are so many still lost. We need to see, hear and feel the tragedy that has been created by the legalization of child killing.

Chapter 3

The Heartbreak

"Joys are our wings;Sorrows our spurs." Jean Paul Richter

"Record my lament; list my tears on Your scrolls – are they not in Your record?"
(Psalm 56:8)

A lone woman staggers out of the killing center. She stops and vomits, sick, in pain and empty. We stand in front, unable to assist in any way. She finally makes it to the car. "Jesus Heals the broken hearted." Is the sign I hold. I wait; sign in one hand, post-abortion information in the other. My heart is filled with tears; tears of sadness, not only for the child whose plan and purpose has been thwarted by the butcher's knife but for this lost, lone, sick woman, who will, for the rest of her life, carry the burden of guilt for the wrong decision made. Unless, silently I pray, "Please Lord, let her take this information. Let her know You love her no matter what." She pulls out of the driveway, I hold the information out to her and we look into each other's eyes. I try to speak love through the tears in mine. She leaves. Without taking the information she just drove away. We pray, "Dear Lord, let her grieve over the loss of her little one. Raise up a Christian that she will talk to."

As useless and hopeless as this appears to be, it is not! This woman saw people who cared, she saw our tears, and she saw the sign. God heard our plea for help and we know that we have done all we could do.

If no one was there who would have prayed for her? If no one was there would she have ever known that the Lord cares, heals, and forgives? - Nancy

For each victory we see there are hundreds of tragedies. For every woman who chooses life for her child there are so many who don't...Why?

Take a good look around. What do you see or hear? The message of sin and death is very prevalent isn't it? Abortion has been legal in our country since 1973. Children have grown up with the concept that abortion is a Constitutional right! Most have come to really believe that it is their Constitutional right to kill a pre-born baby! This perversion of freedom of choice began a slippery downward slide into moral chaos.

This will be addressed further in the last chapter of this book. For now, let us read the testimonies with hearts of compassion for the broken lives, dead babies and destroyed families!

Missing Mary
Dawn shares:

"About two years ago, on a cold Wednesday morning a dark Spanish girl covered in a dark green army jacket walked slowly in front of the abortion clinic on Main St. I approached her and offered her my pro-life literature. To my surprise she took it quite willingly and we talked for quite a while. She thought she was about eight weeks pregnant. She was going in the clinic for a pregnancy test to confirm her fear. If positive she planned on getting an abortion.

As a result of our conversation she agreed to come to my home and take a self-administered pregnancy test that we sometimes offer. It was positive and, according to our calculations, she was indeed almost eight weeks along. We examined every piece of anti-abortion material I had. I explained all the procedures, her options for adoption and showed her all the pictures of fetal development and what happens to the baby in the abortion procedure. Of course, she said she had no idea that this is what abortion really was.

She said she knew our Lord but felt demons were chasing her. Apparently she left her husband and daughter in another nearby town. She felt her husband was into a Satanic Cult. This young woman shared with me that years ago she was diagnosed as a paranoid schizophrenic and was still on heavy medication.

By the time I drove her back to where she was staying she told me that she had decided to keep the baby and keep trusting in the Lord. We prayed together and I asked the Lord to release angels to protect her. For the next two weeks I drove her to the local crisis pregnancy center and got her started in a program that would meet all her needs.

I furnished her barren apartment with all that God had given me to share: food, furniture, glassware and clothes. Each time we met she avoided talking about the baby until I asked. And even after asking I could sense she didn't want to talk about her child.

All along I had a fear that all was not right and when this young lady asked me the very perplexing question, 'Do you think aborted babies go to heaven?' I knew the fear I had been feeling in my heart was grounded in the truth. I said, 'Mary, I believe that they do.' She said quite assuredly, 'I do too and that's why I believe that maybe this baby would be better off in heaven than with me as its mother. I cannot physically or mentally take proper care of this baby, but God can.'

At this time I pleaded with with her, not only to think of her child's life but her own as well. I once again shared with her about the complications of the abortion procedure. I said, 'There is a reason why this baby is growing within you. This child has a plan and purpose set forth by God almighty to have life here on earth. It is not our right to make the decision as to whether that life should be or not be.' I tried to convey to her that adoption would be a very loving solution. We talked and prayed some more and I really felt that we had made some healthy progress. There were many medical needs that I was unqualified to address but, nonetheless, it has always been my policy to fulfill the physical, emotional and spiritual needs of the mothers as much as possible. In Mary's case I felt her needs had not been quite fulfilled. I knew I had done all I could and that the rest was up to the Lord.

Three weeks had passed since I had met Mary. She was now eleven weeks pregnant. According to the social worker that was assigned to Mary through the program she was in, Mary seemed to be emotionally stable. The social worker was truly amazed at how much Mary's self-confidence had improved.

A few days later I went to pick Mary up to take her to her W.I.C. appointment. When I arrived at the apartment she wasn't home. Her sister answered the door and said Mary had an emergency. My heart sank as I thought the worst. She did not have a phone but she did have my phone number. I prayed all night that she would call me. The phone never rang.

The next morning was a rainy, ominous Wednesday. I arrived at the abortion center ready to counsel on the second shift. As I was gathering my packets to pass out, the first shift counselors approached me. I knew something was terribly wrong. They told me they had seen Mary go into the center. I remember the feeling in the pit of my stomach. The pain was indescribable. I stood at the corner, soaked from the torrential rain and my tears blended with the raindrops as they rolled down my cheeks.

Why didn't she call me? Why didn't she talk to me? What stone had I left unturned? Was this baby's life ending because of something I failed to do? These were the thoughts that flooded my mind at that moment and for some time to come.

I gathered the counselors for prayer as I waited for her to come out of that horrible death chamber. Oh Lord, please give her courage to walk out before it's too late. Mary had everything she needed to give her baby life; everything but the confidence in herself as a mother.

My peripheral vision caught a dark green jacket glide by my left side as my head was bowed in prayer. I turned as if in slow motion to see that familiar coat. Our eyes met and held as she was being pulled away by her aunt. She turned back to me and I said, 'Why? Why? Mary, why didn't you call me? You know we could have talked this through.'

She said, 'I am so sorry Dawn. I am so sorry.' As she broke into a heavy sigh, I touched her shoulder in a gentle but firm way; a way I felt Jesus would have touched this troubled, wounded mother. "It's not from me that you need the forgiveness you seek," I said as we locked eyes, once again. As I gently caressed her left arm, her eyes became fixed on the sidewalk in what seemed to be embarrassment and shame.

As she slowly looked up, the last words I said to Mary on the rainy, dark day were, 'I still love you and Jesus still loves you.' Her aunt gave her arm a last tug as she whisked Mary into her car. I prayed, 'Jesus, through this terrible tragedy of abortion a life has ended and left this mother's soul in despair. Have mercy on her as she finds the humility and courage to ask for Your forgiveness. One day she may find salvation and trust in You. Amen.'

I experienced a broken heart that day. I felt so responsible for Mary and her child. But, praise God. He showed me that it was not up to me. It was her choice. He gave me great comfort in knowing I did all that I could do. Although I have never had the opportunity to talk to Mary again I know by faith that Jesus will, and in that truth I have peace."

Our Lord tells us in Matthew 11:28: **"Come to Me, all you who are weary and burdened, and I will give you rest**." And that is where we go in times like this.

Kathy shares this testimony with us:

"One morning while in front of Planned Parenthood praying and hoping to offer pro-life information to the women going in, a woman walked up to me. We struck up a conversation and she proceeded to share with me her abortion experience that took place sixteen years ago. She had been six months pregnant when she went to the abortion center. After the procedure was complete, the "doctor" sarcastically said to her, 'That was your son.'

Grace has since received the Lord's forgiveness and healing but naturally still finds those words painful to think about. She thanked us for being there."

When a conversation such as the one above occurs (and they do often) while we are at the abortion centers, the love of Christ overwhelms us. How wonderfully merciful our Lord is. When we do something so wrong and there is no way to change it or correct it, we can run to Him for forgiveness. When our hearts are so filled with sorrow for others and shame for our country we run to Him and, **"He heals the broken hearted and binds up their wounds." (Psalm 147:3)**

In 1987, in a dumpster behind a local killing center, the tiny bodies of three pre-born babies were found. Little arms with perfect little hands, a leg, part of a head, part of a torso, all about twenty weeks old; children torn apart by the butcher's knife and thrown in the garbage like they were of no value to anyone.

A funeral was held for the children to give them some dignity. When I gazed upon those innocent little human beings my heart broke into a million pieces. What good could possibly come out of aborting innocent babies? There are thousands of decent couples who cannot have children of their own who have to wait years to adopt, and yet we allow this to go on!

Several years ago I was asked to hold a 5-6 month pre-born little girl who was killed by abortion. We had named her Baby Tia. The purpose was to give this beautiful baby dignity and for the pro-lifers to pay their respects and ask God for forgiveness as they filed by. To hold a tiny, perfect human being whose life had a purpose and a reason, but is now dead, was overwhelming. I wept for days after that experience. I think everyone should hold these little ones and see what we are doing in this country.

And the next child shall be born;
Terry shares her testimony:

"I haven't had a save in a long time. However, I am able to hand out information and talk to the moms and dads who are willing to converse. Recently, a dad came out of the abortion center to smoke. I waved him over and shared the salvation message with him. He said they were only there for a check up but I knew that wasn't true. Therefore, I gave him our post-abortion information. He thanked me and went back in. An hour later they both came out. The woman was unable to walk and began vomiting in the parking lot. They went back in again and came out in less than five minutes. As they left I told him to take her to a hospital and he said he would. I thank the Lord that he took all the post-abortion information and I know in my heart that their next child will be born.

We who go to the killing centers have many bittersweet experiences. Sweet because we had the opportunity to touch a heart, perhaps truly help someone meet Jesus and hopefully prevent a repeat abortion. A high percentage of all abortions are repeats. If we can stop the next one, we've done something. Bitter because a child had died, a woman is empty and scarred and a man is helpless because the 'law' states he has no say in the matter.

Too often I have held men in my arms as they wept over the death of their child. Just recently I was at the local abortion center. A young man pulled over, leaped out of his car and asked for signs. His girlfriend was getting an abortion that day at another center. He was shaking all over and extremely distraught. I gave him our literature and told him to get out there. I was sure there were pro-lifers there who would help him. As he was going back to his car I stopped him and prayed for him. May his child have escaped death.

It is totally bizarre that the father has absolutely no say in the decision of whether his child will live or die. Men are being emotionally and spiritually scarred over abortion as deeply as women. The main focus is always on the mother and child and too many times the father is forgotten. Yet, he too must live with the consequences of taking the life of his baby.

Often, at the abortion centers, we see the men sitting in the cars waiting; alone with their thoughts and unable to do anything to stop the death of their child. Yes, many fathers want the abortion; it is the easy out, or so they think. But there are more fathers than we realize that want their baby, would be responsible for their child, weep for what is being done and are helpless to save their son or daughter. They truly are the forgotten fathers."

Sharon shares this:

"One time I was counseling at the abortion center and a couple went in. The man came back out and was very angry. He was a big man and towered over me. Yet, I was filled with the Holy Spirit who is bigger than anyone. He was screaming, spitting and telling me to shut up. I would not. I could not. I knew he needed to hear the truth. Angrily, he walked away and got into his car. I became convicted that I had overstepped the boundary in the things I said and went over to the car to ask for his forgiveness.

When I asked him to forgive me, he turned, looked at me and began to cry. He then got out of the car and shared with me that he did not want this abortion but there was nothing he could do about it. I ended up holding this big man in my arms as he cried in heartbreak over the death of his child.

Forgotten fathers who weep over the children whose touch they will never feel. Lord, forgive us!"

"Too Late," ***submitted by Pat, a sidewalk counselor:***

"About six months ago I witnessed several women coming out of the abortion center. Some women came out with their boyfriends or husbands and some with their friends. Then a few came out by themselves. Some caught taxi cabs and others walked the several blocks to the subway station.

There was one woman in particular, who came out of the center walking very slowly with no one with her. One of the pro-lifers picked up on it and began to follow her. I than saw what was going on and went to assist her.

The woman was African-American (as I am) in her early twenties. When we started talking she was already in denial. She told me that she had no other choice; she had five children at home and couldn't have another baby. She told us that she thought we would call her 'baby killer.' We shared with her that we were not out to judge anyone but instead we were there to offer assistance and the love of Jesus. As we began to gain her trust and put her mind at ease, she felt more comfortable with us. We then offered her a ride home.

I'll never forget that day. It was a cold December afternoon. As this young lady sat in the back seat of my car she began to groan in pain and hold her stomach. I asked if she was alright and she replied,

'I'm hurting and cramping.' I told her to breathe deeply and try to relax, we would have her home soon. I prayed fervently in my heart for the Lord to touch this sad lady.

When we arrived at her apartment, I could sense the hopelessness and despair that she felt as we walked up the dark, dingy stairway. When she opened the door, three beautiful children greeted her. Not five. Her husband or boyfriend stood in the doorway and asked, "Did you do it?" When she nodded her head, he hung his in shame. They both attempted to justify the abortion by saying they had no other choice because they just could not afford another child.

I shared the salvation message with them and gave them information on getting the help they obviously needed. In my heart I knew that if we had been there earlier that day and let her know someone really cared and would help, that child would be alive today. If we had been there this mom and dad would not be in the despair I was witnessing on that December afternoon.

It is my prayer that the Lord would convict more courageous men and women to stand up to speak truth and life to those who are being so deceived."

"If Only," By Kathy:

"We had just started praying and sidewalk counseling at the local Planned Parenthood and I was training a new counselor. A woman approached us and I offered her the literature we give away. She began the conversation with, 'If you had been here five weeks ago, I wouldn't have killed my baby!' She then broke into tears. To sum up her story, the only counseling she had received from P.P. was, "which clinic are you closer to?" That was it.

We arranged follow-up care through a pro-life physician we work with. She is now attending Christian post-abortion counseling. She recently accepted Jesus as her Savior, yet she is still extremely heartbroken over the abortion. Please pray for all the broken women who realize too late.

We all wonder, "How many lives would be saved if more Christians would only pray up, show up and stand up?" Lord, motivate Your Body to action!"

"No One Cares," *from Lisa,*

"It was 9:15 in the morning and I was standing in front of the abortion clinic watching and praying. A car pulled out of the center and stopped for traffic. I walked over to the car and the woman was crying. As tears flowed down her face, her words spilled out on top of each other:

They are so mean and cold in there. They didn't care about how I felt. I tried to tell them I didn't want the abortion; that my husband was forcing me to do it. He threatened to leave me and take my three year old daughter away from me. All they said was, 'get the abortion and we'll send you to a counselor.' Afterwards, they just told me to leave and never did give me a name of anyone to go and talk to. What can I tell my daughter happened to her little brother or sister? I've already had two abortions. I'm twenty-two years old and all I want is a normal life. My mother is a crack addict; I don't have anyone. No one cares…

I put my hand on her shoulder and told her she is not alone anymore. We talked and she took the information on where to go for loving help. When she finally pulled away she knew that someone cares and Jesus loves her."

"Tears," from a faithful counselor:

"One time I went to the local abortion center to pray and sidewalk counsel. On the way there, while I was in prayer, preparing for the battle, the Lord broke my heart. By the time I arrived I was already crying deeply. All I did that morning, at that place of death, is weep on my knees. I couldn't stop crying for the 'little ones' and their parents. Five women walked by me that day and went in. Finally, exhausted, I stood up and left. Later that week I found out that all the women walked out after I left!"

***"Almost,"** from Nancy:*

"She called one evening and said, 'Someone gave me your phone number and said you would help. I'm pregnant and I don't want to be. I'm going to kill myself.'

Silently I prayed, 'Jesus, help me speak life into this woman.'

I cannot write what I said because it was the Holy Spirit speaking through me. Finally, she agreed to meet with me and talk more. The next day we met at the arranged place and I shared more of the love that Jesus gives with her. I told her about the complications of abortion, fetal development and the help that was available.

'I'm in college and I cannot go through with this pregnancy. My mother is dead, my father will not understand and my boyfriend just broke up with me. I did tell him I was pregnant. He said he would pay for the abortion.'

I did my best to convince her not to abort and I promised I would stick with her. That started a three-month relationship that still impacts my life. I set up an appointment with a pro-life OBGYN and she went. When the sonogram was done, it was discovered that she was carrying twins.

Panic set in, along with another suicidal phone call that evening. Again the Lord met me and He convinced her all would be okay. My daughter gave this beautiful young lady all her maternity clothes and my son and his wife, after much prayer, agreed to adopt the twins. It was quickly becoming a family affair. I promised to be a loving grandmother.

However, the boyfriend would not leave her alone. Afraid of child support, he was really pushing her to abort the babies. He hounded her constantly. This man was bold enough to call me and threaten me several times. Her father was not supportive at all and he, too, kept pushing for an abortion. My family was all that stood between life and death for these little ones.

I spoke with her every day. I had her come and stay at my house for a night. We even offered for her to stay in our home until the babies were born. She refused. I tried desperately to get her into Christian counseling. Once again, she refused; saying our friendship and support was all she needed. Phone call after phone call of desperation and despair. She was losing time at school, refusing to take care of herself but continuing with the pregnancy. I invited her to our church; she came once and did not come again.

I sure spent a lot of time on my knees for this young lady and her children. The pregnancy was considered high-risk because she was carrying twins. It was an extremely difficult time for all involved.

Then it seemed like progress was being made. Her attitude became more positive. The phone calls were now upbeat. No longer was suicide an issue, nor did it seem was her boyfriend. We began to really discuss what being a Christian was like. By now she was reading the Bible I gave her and things were starting to look truly hopeful.

She was six months along now and quite big. I thought the babies were safe. I began to plan a baby shower for her and I loved those babies like a grandma should. She asked me to be her coach for the delivery and I was very excited about that.

One evening she called me and said, 'Mom (she had started to call me mom when things became upbeat) I'm going away for a while. I really need to get away from everything. Don't worry, I will take care of myself and the babies, and I'll call you as soon as I get back.'

I truly thought it was alright because she was so far along in the pregnancy and because of the fact that she seemed so very positive about life.

One week later she called me, and I could tell by the sound of her voice that something was terribly wrong.

'I went to New York City and had the abortion. I couldn't take the pressure from my ex-boyfriend anymore. He took me there and paid for everything. Do you hate me now?'

I was in complete shock but I knew I had to say something. 'No, I don't hate you. But more important than what I feel is that Jesus loves you no matter what. Can we meet someplace just to talk?'

She agreed, and later that week we met at 'our' restaurant in the city. I had written her a long letter of love, of heartbreak, of repentance and sorrow for doing what she did. In it were words of the restoration that we can have in Jesus when we truly turn to Him.

It was a very sad meeting. I was still deeply grieving for the little ones and for the consequences this woman would probably suffer from this terribly wrong decision. She was so frail and quiet and her eyes revealed the inner pain she felt. I felt like everything I shared, did and stood for meant nothing in the final decision.

I gave her the letter. We talked a little. I held her hand and told her I loved her, and we parted. I never saw her again.

I tried to call but the number was changed. I even went to her house but her and her father had moved. To this day I feel as if it were my grandchildren that died. I have prayed often for this young lady I learned to love. And I take comfort that when I get to heaven I'll get to meet my two adopted twins.

It is times like these when our hearts truly cry out to the Lord for answers. It is times like these His Holy Words give great comfort. Psalm 34:18 tells us, 'The Lord is close to the brokenhearted and saves those who are crushed in spirit.' Faith takes on a new dimension as it really becomes the assurance of things hoped for; as we hold tightly to His love and promises. Slowly, through the tears, through the pain, we become convicted of things not seen. His ways are **not** ours, and He is fully in control, no matter how it looks.

We are refined with the fire of tragedy and we begin to see the suffering that our Lord Jesus went through when He walked on the earth. Does faith waver? No, this was her choice. This tragedy was of her own doing. Our Lord was, and will continue to be, there to love her, forgive her and help her. This young lady shut the door of her heart and He will wait for her to open it and let Him in.

I did my best. I offered her truth, love and assistance in any way she needed. Do I understand why she succumbed to the pressure applied by her ex and her father? No, I don't, and I also know I won't until I see our Lord face to face. We cry, we wonder, we press into His love more than ever and He meets us. The Lord renews our determination and we keep on keeping on!"

"Please Help My Daughter," ***from Gloria:***

"The phone rang. It was a lady from Pennsylvania asking for help. Her daughter, a college student, was on her way to an abortion center near me. She had just found out about it and was trying to stop her daughter. This woman was beside herself with grief and she was pleading with me to do everything possible to stop her grandchild from being killed.

I received the description of the young lady and as many details as I could to try to figure out which abortion center she was going to. We prayed together and then I got busy lining up counselors to find this young mom.

We did find out where she was and we did have the opportunity to talk to her. She was adamant in her decision to have the abortion. This pregnancy was not going to interfere with her education. We told her that it would not. We told her of the possibility of complications, emotionally and physically. She was still determined.

Everything that could be done was done.
She had the abortion anyway.

"I stayed in contact with the grandmother and gave her phone numbers of several post-abortion counselors. What heartbreak; this grandmother felt the loss of her grandchild deeply. Eventually, so did the mom; she ended up with severe post-abortion syndrome and dropped out of college. Now, receiving intense counseling, may she receive our Lord's forgiving love.

Now, a dear friend of mine, Betty, has become involved in the pro-life movement in Pennsylvania and had dedicated her life to letting college students know the dangers of abortion. Let us never forget: for every child aborted there are grandparents who are also wounded; their silent tears go unnoticed.

The following are two testimonies that are from the mother's point of view. They share the tragedy of abortion and the restoring love of Jesus. May all of us come to the true awareness of how damaging legalized abortion really is. And may the Christians recognize how important it is to share the love and healing grace of our Lord to everyone we meet. We all need to realize that millions of men and women are suffering in silence as they carry the burden of such a wrong decision.

"Young and Alone," ***name withheld:***

"I was fifteen years old; alone, frightened and four months pregnant. I had no one to talk to as I had a terrible relationship with my family and was very rebellious. I went to Planned Parenthood. They referred me to a hospital in a nearby city. They told me everything would be ok; that I would go to this hospital, it would take a few hours and my problem would be solved.

Well, that sounded great! I felt good about taking care of "my problem" quickly and no one would ever know about it. I was pretty naïve and did not really know anything about being pregnant. I only knew that I didn't want to be pregnant, and I was given what I thought to be a good solution. After all, I was told that only good would come out of the abortion. What did I have to lose except some trouble?

The morning came for my appointment and I arrived at the hospital a little nervous. I had been told it was a simple procedure and that it wouldn't take long; that I'd be back to normal by the afternoon... and I believed that.

As I sat in the waiting room I became very uneasy and upset. A nurse spoke to me and explained very briefly what was going to happen: "We will take a little fluid out of your uterus and put a solution in. You will experience a little cramping and then pass some tissue. After resting a while you can go home."

I started to cry. I didn't know why, but the tears kept coming. The nurse (who never once looked directly at me) asked, "Are you sure you want to do this?"

I said, 'I guess so.'

Then I was led into a room with a bed and a bathroom. Someone came in, neither of us talked, and he put a long needle into by abdomen and took some fluid out. It really hurt. Then he injected something into me, turned and walked out. I was alone and terrified.

I closed my eyes and wished I would die. My heart was pounding within my chest and I knew there was no turning back. Soon after the injection I began to get bad cramps and felt like my stomach was jumping all over the place. The pain got real bad. Then I felt like I had to move my bowels. It got off the bed and something came out of me. I looked down and between my legs a perfect tiny baby hung by the cord; dead and burned, a little girl. Horrified, I screamed and the nurse ran in immediately.

Sitting on the floor looking at the baby I became completely blank. I said nothing, I felt nothing. The placenta came out, then the nurse cleaned me up and said, "You're finished now. Rest a while, then you can go home." An hour later I left the hospital.

Never looking back I achieved total denial before I was out the door. No one told me, no one explained, no one comforted me and for many, many years I buried this secret.

For years I lived with my nightmares of babies crying, of dead babies floating in and out of my sleep. Then the pro-life movement became visible and little bits of truth about abortion started to penetrate the wall I had built. It was then I faced my nightmare. It was then that I met Jesus Christ as my Lord and Savior and His grace started to work in me. I admitted to myself that I had killed my baby and I asked the Lord to forgive me. He did, and that's when I began to forgive myself. Yes, I can justify my decision by my own ignorance, by the fact that I was lied to and that I was not told the facts. But the truth is the final decision and the consequences are mine. I have even forgiven those who did not tell me the truth. I cannot bring my daughter back but now I know where she is and I know that someday I will see her again, and in that I have peace."

Abortion leaves one dead and many wounded. We as Christians are responsible for caring for the wounded. His Word is clear on this. Take the time to read Luke 10: 25-37.

This next testimony, which will also go unnamed, is from a sidewalk counselor whose love for Jesus shines from her life like a beautiful sunrise. Furthermore, as a sidewalk counselor she is able to relate to the women going in for an abortion. She is very effective at the abortion centers. It is an honor to print her story.

"He Never Leaves Me..."

"My mother always said I was a miracle baby. She wanted another girl but the doctors said she would die if she got pregnant again. She prayed for four years to have another girl anyway. And God answered her prayers. The pregnancy and delivery were very difficult, but the Lord came through and I was born. I knew at a very young age that the Lord's Hand had caused me to be born in spite of the hard circumstances. It gave me a sense that He had a plan for my life.

As a child I loved the Lord and loved to hear all the Bible stories. I accepted Jesus as my Savior at the age of seven. I knew that He made me clean and I was forgiven. However, as I grew up many things happened. Being the youngest in a very large family was very difficult at times. Furthermore, my self-image was not very good. There was a deep desire to be accepted and loved by those around me. I now know that this happened because I thought more of what others thought of me than I did about what the Lord thought of me. Therefore, the Lordship of Jesus was slowly being replaced by a 'me' lordship.

By now I was a very rebellious teenager. I was involved in the rock n roll culture of that time. My rebellion climaxed at the age of seventeen. It was then I found out I was pregnant. I had just graduated from high school and thought I had my whole life before me. This was not part of the plan. I was in extreme turmoil to say the least! For many weeks I denied the thought that I was pregnant. I didn't want all the fun to end.

I am too young, I thought. My parents will be so upset. What will our church say? I asked some friends what to do. One of them told me abortion was wrong but offered no explanation. I was feeling very alone and frightened. It was then I prayed to God to tell me if an abortion was the right thing. I clearly heard Him say, "No," yet I was so far into my rebellion that I still chose to do my own thing.

I turned my back on God and had an abortion when I was eleven and half weeks pregnant. I deceivingly convinced myself that I was being brave and strong by doing such a thing. The staff at the clinic helped me to focus on myself and not on my baby or what I was doing.

I remember the doctor would not look at me. I thought that was very strange, especially in the light of the fact that abortion is a good solution to a bad problem.

It was over very quickly and I decided to be tough; I was in denial.

After this my life seemed to go back to normal; however, very quickly things started to go out of control. I was partying and being promiscuous more than ever. I had a hard time being around any of my young nieces and nephews and children in general. I had been accepted to a local college and had received grants for the government. Even with that incentive I did not go. I had no direction in my life and I knew I would apply myself to study. Depression was my constant companion.

At age nineteen, I had an offer to go to Florida with some friends. I left my home town and started a new life down there. Away from my old friends, family and memories the Lord started to tug at my heart. I was getting oh so tired of the things of this world and I was remembering my Lord.

One day, while reading a Christian magazine, I came across an article on abortion. It explained what really happens in an abortion procedure such as the one I underwent.

I learned that day that my baby was fully developed. I learned what the suction machine did to her; how it had severed, tore and crushed her little body. I was horrified.

I had chosen to do this to my baby. I realized that I was a mother now, but of a dead baby. I was overwhelmed with remorse. I think I knew it all the while in my heart. Now I could no longer deny it. This was the beginning of my healing. Seeing and knowing the true facts of my actions broke through the barrier of denial that I had been living with for so long.

I asked the Lord for forgiveness. I also went home for a while and confessed to my mother what I had done. I asked her to forgive me, and she did. With that, forgiveness for me began to grow. It was then that I re-dedicated my life back to the Lord.

Shortly after this, I married a wonderful man. It was then that I became involved in pro- life activity and began to sidewalk counsel. Even so, God was not done with my healing yet.

One evening I was preparing to go to a pro-life meeting at our church. I was breastfeeding our second daughter and admiring how beautiful her little hands were. God had created her so wonderfully. I was a little anxious about this meeting as there was to be an aborted baby in a jar of formaldehyde for us to see. I had seen all the pictures and read all the facts on abortion but had not yet seen an aborted baby. I felt the Lord wanted me to have a close look, but I was hesitant. At the end of the meeting I finally made myself look at the baby in the jar.

Head crushed and body torn apart, a little girl floated in silence. She was between twelve and thirteen weeks old. But what touched my heart the most is her hands were still in tact and they were beautiful. They looked exactly like my baby daughters hands, just smaller. It was all just too much. A flood of emotions hit me like a ton of bricks. I saw the filthiness of my soul as never before. Yet, at the same time the Spirit of the Lord showed me the awesome price He paid for my soul. Jesus died for my sins. He knew that I would commit horrible and despicable sins. But He did it anyway to save me. I realized, with a greater degree of understanding, the love Jesus has for me. His love is immeasurable. It was almost too much for me to bear. I left the meeting and drove home crying tears of healing and tears of love. My God was mighty and loved me enough to die in my place.

I now have four beautiful daughters here on earth and two beautiful children in heaven, as I also had a miscarriage. I think often about the child I lost to abortion and wonder what could have been. I look forward to the day when we will be a complete family in heaven.

When I had turned my back on God, He never left me but instead brought me back to His heart. What the enemy desired for evil in my life, our Lord turned around for good. He had, and has, a plan for my life because He promised, **"He who began a good work in me and He will be faithful to complete it." (Philippians 1:6, paraphrased)**

It is in the darkest hour that our Lord meets us with the intensity of His love. In that moment of time when Jesus hung on the Cross, His Father looked away and all the sin of the world, from the beginning to the end, was poured out on Him. It appeared to be the darkest span of time in existence, and yet it was the most wonderful, glorious light-bearing moment of grace that ever has been, or will be, in the world we now know.

For in the willingness, in the love, in the pain, and in the sorrow we were freed!

In our darkest hour at the abortion centers, when baby after baby is brutally slaughtered, when woman after woman is maliciously exploited and nothing we do seems to change that. These are the times when the Lord meets us, strengthens us, saves our tears and lets us know how much He loves us.

In the darkest hour of an aborted woman, when the walls come down and she faces what she has done, He is there to heal, comfort and forgive. It is the same for the fathers and the grandparents. No one is beyond His love, His blood and His forgiveness.

It is an exercise in futility to be angry or frustrated. It is an exercise of faith to press in, press on and trust the Lord. Those of us who go out experience the heartbreak that exists in such abundance, and we never forget. I think often of the young women who called me 'mom' and of the 'twin grandchildren' I almost had. Yet in my thinking, the Lord comforts me with His peace. And we cling to the Scripture that says,

> *"Those who sow in tears will reap with songs of joy. He who goes out weeping, carrying seed to sow, will return with songs of joy, carrying sheaves with him." (Psalm 126:5-6)"*

Chapter 4

Defeats That Were Not

"So is My word that goes out from My mouth: It will not return to Me empty, but will accomplish what I desire and achieve the purpose for which I sent it." (Isaiah 55:11)

If we knew of all the victories that are being wrought in heaven and here on earth, because the Lord rewarded our faithfulness, we would become puffed up and boastful. Our old nature demands attention; it craves accolades and praise. We were all created to give praise, worship and love to God the Father. But when Satan said, "You will be like God, knowing good and evil" (Genesis 3:5b). We willfully disobeyed God and did what Satan encouraged us to do. I say us and not Adam and Eve because we still do the same thing today, don't we? How many times have we known to do right but gave into the wrong?

I know for myself I've chosen the wrong over the right more times than I care to admit. I also know that we naturally will take credit for the things we do right. Therefore, understanding this principle, if we saw all the saves that our Lord uses us in we would take the credit and bathe ourselves in the praise. This is not acceptable to the Father.

So many times we stand, pray, cry, and plead at the abortion centers for hours at a time and nothing appears to happen. Those times are real faith builders where real trust comes in and we rely on Isaiah 55:

11 for comfort. Then our shift ends and all we have experienced is the staff mocking us, the women yelling at us, the police ordering us around and the people driving by swearing at us We know the Lord wants us to be there, the women need us and the little ones, whose silent cries cannot be heard, require our presence. Yet it sure can be a dark rainstorm.

Sometimes at the end of a rainstorm a rainbow is seen. Its beauty is breathtaking and we are filled with the awesome wonder of God's creation. As the colors blend together in intensity and arch in their beauty across the sky, we are filled with hope; hope for a brighter tomorrow, strength to get through today and remembrance of blessings gone by!

From Kay, a sidewalk counselor for many years:
A Rainbow of Thanksgiving

"I heard that a local mission was in need of diapers. My partner and I went out and purchased several boxes. On the way to deliver them I said to my friend, 'In all the times I've been at the abortion centers counseling, I've never seen a save that I was instrumental in.'

When we walked into the mission kitchen, a mom with a toddler on her hip was standing there. The woman kept staring at me. After a brief conversation the woman said to me,

'You were passing out information on High street a few years ago, weren't you?'

"Yes," was my answer. "Well," the woman replied, "You would not give up on trying to give me information and I finally took it. You changed my mind and my daughter is here now because of you!"

The toddler stood in front of me for a moment and then ran back to mom. My eyes filled with tears, my heart with gratefulness. The Lord, in His love for me, let me see that I do not go in vain!"

How many hearts have been touched as moms and dads drove by the abortion centers and saw our signs that say, "Jesus Heals the Brokenhearted," and, "Let Your Baby Live We Will Help You"? How many minds have been changed by seeing the picture of a beautiful eight week old pre-born baby that we hold while out there? How many babies have been saved by the heartfelt witness of seeing us there praying, praying and praying some more? How many people have drawn strength and determination by seeing our steadfastness? How many ministries have been started because someone saw us at the centers, week after week, month after month and year after year? Perhaps they said, "If they can do that, then I can do this."

The Lord has shown us enough rainbows that we know we are being effective but not so many that we would become puffed up. Furthermore, we will never know it all in this life but we take our assurance again and again from His Holy Word:

> *"For the Son of Man is going to come in his Father's glory with his angels and then he will reward each person according to what he has done." (Matthew 16:27)*

"And a Rainbow Filled My Soul!" ***by Nancy:***

"In 1990 I was in jail for being an active Christian. I was privileged to serve the Lord while I was there. I had many opportunities to witness the salvation message and give His love away. Many of the women there did accept Jesus as Savior. However, one particular lady stands out in my memories. She was a drug addict since her early teens.

Her life was one of tragedy and despair. Anna (not her real name) had become a prostitute in order to support her habit at a very young age. Anna also had an abortion and lived in confusion and hopelessness. I did as the Lord directed and spent a lot of time sharing His Word with her.

Then I was released. I attempted to stay in contact with her to no avail. Three years later I ran into one of the guards I got to know while in jail. It was then I found out this young lady became pregnant after being released but chose life for her child, had the baby and gave him up for adoption. Later still, I found out that she committed her life to Jesus and is finally on the right path.

Our Lord's timing is rarely ours. We, in America, are 'McDonald Christians.' We want to drive through and see instant victory. The Lord does not always respond to our faithfulness instantly. *Instantly* is not a product of faith. A rainbow only comes after a storm."

Then there was the literature blitz:
Colors of Love, Rainbows of Hope

"Several years ago, we did a campaign to pass out pro-life information along with salvation tracts in a neighborhood near an abortion center. We went door to door passing out packets. One of the volunteers knocked on a door and when it was opened, she could see a little girl standing in the hall.

The woman who opened the door said, 'Do you know a nun who stands outside an abortion center on Linwood?' It just happened that this pro-lifer did know Sister Mary.

The lady then said, "Over two years ago this nun was at this center and her presence changed my daughter's mind. Here is my granddaughter, and I thank God for her!"

For over two years Sister Mary did not know how powerfully the Lord worked through her. Needless to say, Sister Mary received a very happy phone call that day."

Fruit of Faithfulness

"It was Wednesday morning and we were at the local abortion center. Usually it is a very busy morning and we were prayed up and ready to do our best. A car pulled up and we approached it to counsel the woman driving.

'No!' the lady laughed, 'I'm not going in. I just stopped by to show you the product of your faithfulness. You changed my mind over a year ago and here is my beautiful daughter.'

In the back seat was a little girl about eight months old, smiling like a little sunbeam! The mom then said, 'I am now attending church regularly, love the Lord and thank you for being here. Could I have some of your literature to pass out at church and where I work?'

Well folks, we just stood there and our hearts were just filled with love. The Lord showed us a victory we knew nothing about. We gave that mom enough literature to last a long time!" – The counselors from Linwood.

Here are some quotes that were joy to our ears, food for our souls and rainbows of light to our hearts:

'I saw you people standing here and I had to stop and say thank you. A year ago my girlfriend was going in here for an abortion. You talked her out of it. My child is the joy of my life!'

'I saw your signs and changed my mind.'

'I told God, if someone was standing in front of the abortion clinic, I wouldn't go in.' (This happens a lot)

What a privilege it is to serve the King!"

From Kathy, a double rainbow!

"On March 14th, we had our first confirmed save due to our efforts. On that day, during my shift, I met an eighteen year old mom. She introduced me to her eight week old daughter, Makayla, who was spared from the abortion because of a packet of information she took from us a year ago. It was a thrilling experience. All I can say is Keep your eyes on the Prize; hold on!

We had news of a second baby saved due to our efforts: One of the sidewalk counselors spoke to a young mother while at Planned Parenthood on July 20th. Another little girl! The mom said the information we gave her changed her mind and her daughter is now ten months old."

Larry shares with us:

A few months back, a young fellow pulled into the abortion clinic's parking lot. He came over to us and showed us a picture of a young toddler. His wife wanted to abort the baby but after much discussion he talked her out of it. Now, they can't imagine their life without their child. He said to us, 'Never stop doing what you are doing. You have no idea how much good you are accomplishing!'

I often think about the children that have been saved from the abortionist's knife. They now have the opportunity to be all that the Lord intended them to be. 'Hope for a brighter tomorrow, strength for today, remembrance of blessings gone by.'"

One final testimony that speaks to the truth of our physical presence being effective whether we ever see the results or not:

"A young woman stopped with her new daughter. She wanted to tell us how happy she was that we were out in front of the abortion center. Her boyfriend's cousin worked inside of this particular center. By remembering seeing us, the young lady knew abortion was wrong. She called the clinic to make her boyfriend happy. The secretary at the clinic told her it would cost $350.00 and said, "Don't go to your own doctor." This young mom also told us that if we weren't there she would have let her boyfriend talk her into the abortion. Even though we never spoke to her, just our presence was enough. Then she said she had some needs and asked if we would we help her?

We were able to supply her with food and clothing. The Lord had given us a chance to show her and her boyfriend that we really are sincere. The boyfriend was shocked and touched that we truly care. We all just praise God for the opportunities that He gives us to share His love." Eileen

Thank You, Lord, for Your rainbows of love and life!

Chapter 5

The Cost

"...Therefore, whether declaring God's truth against Satan's falsehoods or in taking up the protection of the good and innocent against the wrongs of the wicked, we must undergo the offenses and hatred of the world, which may imperil either our life, our fortunes, or our honor." –*John* Calvin

One of the most misunderstood aspects of the pro-life Christian activities is why so many of us went to jail. Did we break the law? Furthermore, does going to prison make a difference?

The majority of people wrongly assume that when a Christian pro-lifer goes to jail in the U.S.A., they've broken the law. Most people make the assumption that America is still free, fair and honorable. It is very difficult to truly recognize just how corrupt and morally decadent the United States has become. As a matter of fact, we have compromised our integrity and honor to such a degree, over such a long period of time, that we don't want to recognize what we've become.

Noah Webster's definition of *compromise*: "To adjust and settle a difference by mutual agreement, with concessions of claims by the parties." Look around and think about all the Christian principles we have conceded in order to be part of our communities, our academic systems and our work environment.

Furthermore, because our country is on such shifting sand we live in fear for our economy and our social stability. As a matter of fact, to move off the shifting sand onto the solid Rock now takes a great deal of courage and a willingness to be rejected. After all, a move back into Christian integrity and moral ethics with a firm stand to really be who we are supposed to be in Christ - His ambassadors to a sick and dying world - causes us to really take the risk of losing finances and being rejected by friends and family. We take the risk of being falsely accused, misunderstood and even possibly put in jail. People are now finding it very difficult to believe that Jesus Christ really takes care of His own.

A very interesting fact is that we sympathize, pray for, and help financially, those who are put in prison or beaten in China and other countries where Christianity is oppressed. We say, "What heroes... what people of faith!" And their heroism inspires us to send more Bibles, more support, more prayers, more fasting. Rightly so; it is one hundred percent correct.

However, when a pro-life Christian goes to jail in America for standing up for Christ, the pre-born babies and their mothers, we frown and say, "They're too radical!" A double standard perhaps? Or is it just plain denial of the truth of what is really happening in our country?

When a pro-lifer gets arrested for saving babies or preaching the Gospel in front of a place where innocent pre-born babies are being slaughtered, do the majority of people, Christian and non-Christian, say, "What people of faith!"? Or do they say, "They broke the law, there must be another way, and worst of all; that's not being a real Christian."?

It's one thing to be hated and persecuted by the world but it sure is extremely hurtful to be persecuted by those who call themselves Christians. It's one thing for the world to be silent about the millions of babies, now dead, and the men and women scarred; it's another for the church, whose voice is supposed to be heard, to be silent.

If the church had really stood up when rescue was at its peak, I believe that abortion would be a sin of the past. Instead, today, 32% of Planned Parenthood's income comes from killing pre-born babies. Instead, we now are lusting after embryonic stems cells with a vengeance. Instead, we now are legalizing same-sex marriages in many states. I could go on and on but I think the point is made. As I stated previously, "the proof is in the pudding." All we need to do is look around and compare the today of 2007 to the yesterday of 1959. We're not only on a slippery slope; we are careening downward at a rapid speed. Yet, I believe this all could be changed for the good, with unity and determination. I will address that in the last chapter.

If we were not about our Father's business then why has the world been so intense in their quest to stop Christians who stand publicly for the truth? Just look at the injunctions, acts of Congress and laws that have been created to stop us! Active pro-life Christians are hated by the world, of this there is no doubt.

"All men will hate you because of Me, but he who stands firm to the end will be saved." (Matthew 10:22)

Here's an important fact: when I "locked in" (went right inside an abortion center and locked myself to others so they couldn't open the center) I knew I would go to jail. I knew that I was breaking man's law and "criminally trespassing." I knew the cost was high. And I knew I was obeying the Lord's command to protect the fatherless. What it cost me, both times, was ninety days in jail. What it saved was God's children; children that would live the life that the Lord ordained! I did not "lock in" without counting the cost.

What I am saying is those of us who rescued during the 80's and 90's knew there was a price to pay and we were willing to pay it.

However, when I was continuously arrested for standing on a public sidewalk and offering help to a mom in crisis, well, that was just plain hatred and outright greed by the pro-aborts.

Furthermore, the courts went along with the false accusations. It took a great deal of self-discipline not to get angry for being treated so unjustly. Then we would remember what Jesus did for us. We would remember that many Christians across the world suffer so much for their faith, and our anger would disappear.

The war for our lives was won at the Cross. Satan was defeated, and the keys of death and hell were taken from him. The price for our sin was paid for by our Lord Jesus and our eternal life with the Father is guaranteed to those who believe. Yet, until all have had the opportunity to hear, and choose, the battle rages on.

In World War Two, on June 6, 1944, the invasion of Normandy began. That strategy and invasion basically won the war in Europe. Hitler knew he was defeated. Did he give up then? No, the war raged on in Europe for another year!

So it is in the spiritual realm. Satan knows he lost. He knows his time is limited. But he will continue to lie, confuse, and kill the innocent through the sinful nature of man. He will continue to break down mankind on every front so as to take as many people as he can to hell with him. He knows how to break the heart of our Lord.

In the years I've been a pro-life missionary, I have witnessed more demonic attacks at abortion centers than anywhere else I've ever been. I have also witnessed the power and moving of the Holy Spirit with intensity that far surpasses anything else I've ever experienced!

In my missionary work I have spent over a year in jail. Not all together; five months at one prison, three months at another, days and weeks at several different ones. Each and every time it was for standing (or sitting) for Jesus, the little ones who are completely defenseless, and their parents. Hundreds of pro-life Christians have been imprisoned for this very reason. This is our testimony. This is our witness of the awesome love, grace and comfort Jesus gives when His children are brought before the court system and put in jail for being obedient to His Word.

I have been arrested, put in jail and severely fined for praying on a public sidewalk, playing a cassette with a ten week pre-born baby's heartbeat, and for speaking to women going into the abortion center (as far as a block away!). I have had my signs of truth and love taken away from me because I set them down on the ground. I was arrested after an abortionist body slammed me against a brick wall and then lied to the police, who never questioned him or listened to me.

We did the right, we showed the Light! And the corrupt people in positions of power say, "You can't do that."

In the early church, Christians went to prison and were martyred because they would not compromise the truth: "Jesus is Lord, we will not bow our knee to another." It is no different now. We were not persecuted and sent to prison for saving the babies. It happened because our actions stated, very clearly, that Jesus is Lord; Lord of life, Lord of freedom, Lord of all! By our actions we exposed the despicable evil that is still present in our country. This does not win a popularity contest.

The Apostle Paul questioned in Galatians 4:16, "Have I now become your enemy by telling you the truth?" The answer is yes. We caused people to be uncomfortable. And in today's culture people will do anything to stay comfortable. It's even to the point where Christians will blind their hearts to the truth that abortion sheds innocent blood and that we all should do something about it.

Did we want to go to prison? Absolutely not! We were willing to go because we were obedient to His calling us to defend the defenseless.

I have been in court because of my faith many, many times. Each time it has unquestionably been a witness for Jesus. The last time I was in court, I was facing a ten count indictment for violating a federal injunction. After much praying the decision was made to represent myself in court. During that trial the Lord made it possible for me to give the whole salvation message to everyone in the courtroom under oath as His witness. Not one person who was there can ever say they didn't hear the Good News about our Lord Jesus!

Anyone that goes to court to receive their sentence after being found guilty is allowed to make a statement before the sentence is handed down by the judge. Many pro-lifers take this opportunity to witness truth. The following is an excerpt from a statement of a godly pro-life, elderly gentleman as he was being sentence to jail for sitting at the front door of an abortion center:

...My grandfather was a judge on the bench for thirty-six years as a circuit court county judge. My father was a judge also; he too served for thirty-four years. ... So I respect the law.... Abraham Lincoln, before he became President, in a series of debates with Steven Douglas, talked about the moral issue of his day, which we all know was slavery. In his most famous debate with Douglas, his, *A House Divided,* speech he did not call on the Constitution for his moral position. He called upon the Declaration of Independence. The Constitution, as interpreted by the Supreme Court of that day, was upholding the institution of human bondage.

But what does the Declaration of Independence have to say? The Declaration of Independence is the American creed. It states the things in which we believe, just as the Apostle's Creed states the beliefs of Christians.

So, in this court I think I would like to recall to us the opening lines of the Declaration of Independence:

When, in the course of human events, it becomes necessary for one people to dissolve the political bonds which have connected them to another, and to assume among the powers of the earth, the separate and equal station to which the laws of nature and of nature's God entitle them, a decent respect to the opinions of mankind requires that they should declare the causes which impel them to the separation.

We hold these truths to be self-evident, that all men are created equal, that they are endowed by their Creator with certain unalienable rights, that among these are life, liberty and the pursuit of happiness.

That to secure these rights, governments are instituted among men, deriving their just powers from the consent of the governed.

That whenever any form of government becomes destructive to these ends, it is the right of the people to alter or abolish it."

Well, what does the Declaration of Independence have to say about the issue to which we are dedicated, ending the shedding of innocent blood?

First of all, it says we are created equal. But what does created mean? We are created when we come into existence, and each of us came into existence at the moment of conception, not nine months later. We are not being created equal when one third of human beings in this country are not allowed to live while the other two thirds are. That is not equality.

We are endowed by our Creator with the unalienable rights of life, liberty and the pursuit of happiness. There is a reason for that order. You cannot pursue happiness unless you have liberty, and you cannot have liberty unless you are alive. The abortionists prevent the pursuit of happiness. One group is being allowed the pursuit of happiness over the right to life of another. The unborn children lose not just the right to live, but all the rights. They have no liberty and no happiness if they have no life. So they lost all of their liberties. This government was instituted to protect those rights. It says that if any form of government... that is destructive of those ends, it is the right of the people to alter or abolish that government. It states later in the Declaration that it is not only a right, but a duty.

...In the last days of his life, Thomas Jefferson wrote, "When I realize that God is a just God, I fear for the future of my country." He was speaking on the subject of slavery when he said, "Every drop of blood drawn by the lash may be shed on the battle field." Years later we had the Civil War. There were more casualties in that war than in all the other wars put together. God's justice prevailed.

And in this war on the unborn there are millions upon millions of dead babies. Their blood is crying up to heaven for justice, and at some point in our history their cry for justice will drown out the cry for mercy that we rescuers ask of our Lord. ...Our constant prayer is to ask Christ to shed His mercy on America, to turn us away from what we do. ...I fear if this destruction of our pre-born is not brought to justice, our country will not survive as the United States of America as we know it and our founding father's set up for us to enjoy.

Therefore, faced with a choice of trespassing at what I call an abortion slaughter house or trespassing on our founding national charter, The Declaration of Independence, the American creed, I state, to not trespass on the former would be to trespass on the latter.

...I'll finish with this: the Declaration of Independence is listed first in the code of the United States Statutory Law. It is organic law in this country and it is not being enforced. It was not enforced in Lincoln's time either. Therefore, I am not breaking the law in what I did. I am trying to uphold the law, exercising my right, my duty...my duty as stated in the Declaration of Independence...to secure their God-given rights of life, liberty and the pursuit of happiness. – Dr. Terrance

Dr. Terrance made a lot of sense, didn't he? Hundreds of Christians not only counted the cost but indeed felt it was their duty to rescue the babies. However, the hardships became very serious. Some pro-lifers lost their homes the costs became very high. The wonderful, honorable lawyers helping us worked over time for only rewards in heaven. Everyone who stood up or sat down for life paid a huge price.

Chapter 6

And We Paid!

Prison is just like any other mission field with two very important differences: we do not have a choice and we do not want to go. However, once we are there it is amazing how the Lord meets us, works through us and causes us to mature in Him. I pray with all my heart that the following word picture of Christians in prison will touch your heart. We stand before you now and show you our hearts.

Surrendering...

In the quiet place of our hearts we surrender all to our Lord. While waiting to be taken we are surrounded by our loved ones; words of encouragement touch our ears, tears of sadness touch our spirits and then it happens: "Time to go," and we are taken away. We are separated from our families and normal life. Yet, Jesus never leaves us...we can never be taken from Him!

In the natural...

Going to prison is a violation of the mind, emotions and of physical well being. Your modesty is violated in the strip searches. In some prisons you are sprayed for lice. It is a rape of all physical senses; the noise is deafening and never ending. The obscene language is offensive, the lights are always on and you are deprived of any physical expression of affection. It is a hard and lonely discipline to not be hugged or kissed for long periods of time. You become a number in the system, no name, no personal identity. True privacy is non-existent. All rules must be obeyed without question and they change constantly. Most of the rules are created to intimidate and break your spirit. Severe punishment does occur if you do break a rule and the guards are always looking for you do to so.

The sleeping quarters are usually extremely uncomfortable and it is either too hot or too cold. Medical care in prison is deplorable. Food, in most of the prisons I've been in, is barely palatable. You have no choices. You make no decisions and, if in for a prolonged period of time, you become institutionalized, mentally and emotionally. In essence, you become a non-person with no identity, no freedom, and being treated unfairly, unjustly and without respect. There is physical, mental and emotional abuse in prison that can and does damage inmates for life.

In the spiritual:

Paradoxically, going to prison for Christ is the most spiritually uplifting, maturing and productive experience a Christian can walk through! We feel humbled to have been counted worthy to suffer for Him. We are thankful that we did what He asked us to do, honored that we have the opportunity to be His ambassadors behind prison walls. And always, the sense of His Presence becomes strong and true.

In the awareness of His Presence we see the babies who are torn apart, painfully killed under the banner of "safe and legal," and we thank Him that babies were saved by our actions. We feel the hurt of the women who have gone through the abortion procedure. These women have become de-sensitized, physically wounded, emotionally scarred and spiritually hardened because of the perversion of freedom of choice! How then, can we be indignant over a little hardship that lasts only for a season? Within all this realization Jesus gives us His grace to walk through the "time"! Furthermore, the opportunities to witness and minister His love and truth are beyond calculation.

The reality:

I would be remiss if I did not share that our emotions and thoughts do run high and low. We do feel anger because of the unfairness. We do feel deep loneliness for our loved ones, especially when we are far from home. We feel deep sorrow for our silent churches. And yet, we feel honored to share God's love with the lost and we feel deep sorrow when we hear their stories. Our old nature suffers and our spiritual one grows in leaps and bounds!

My experience in jail ranged from being in maximum security jails to minimum security jails, and even to federal prison camp. Maximum security jails are very strict and very guarded. They have men with machine guns walking on the roof every night, very little outdoor time, restricted visiting, and physical abuse. Minimum security jails are less guarded but have crazier rules. They have less physical abuse but more mental abuse. Federal prison camps have low security, few guards, no locks and no cells; they just little (very little) "cubes." However, the camp had very strict rules and any breaking of the rule of the day was met with severe punishment. Each jail experience was unique, intense and maturing.

It all started:

In the fall of 1987, I went to Cherry Hill, New Jersey to "rescue the babies." It was very scary because it was the first time I put my body, my life, on the line for someone else.

An assembly was held the night before the actual rescue. All of us who were willing to sit in front of the abortion center doors had to sign a non-violent contract. It stated that we promised not to react in any violent manner to the police or anyone else. We were to let ourselves be dragged away silently in order to identify with the little ones whose voices cannot be heard.

That night we prayed together and honestly prepared to lay our lives down to stop the killing. This was the first national rescue and we did not know what would happen.

Each of us was given a Psalter (old time song and prayer book). Then it was morning; time to go. With hearts pounding, we silently walked to the place where they kill innocent babies and exploit women, and sat down. With heads bowed and hearts grieving, we prayed, we sang God's songs and we locked arms in hope that we would wake up this country, save children and have the opportunity to help women in crisis. The police came, the pro-abortion people came, the media came and the place closed down.

One by one we were dragged away, in silence and tears. We were handcuffed and placed on a bus. We had no idea what would happen to us. Yet there was a joy that filled our souls. No babies died that day and we learned later that a few moms changed their minds and received good and positive help!

In the end nothing really happened to us. We were released and no one was charged.

However, all that changed as we became more effective and noticed. We were touching a sick, sore spot across our country. We were making the invisible visible, and most people didn't like it.

Thousands of Christians began to join us and soon rescues were taking place in front of many abortion centers. The abortionists were losing business, the politicians were getting nervous and the mainstream media was busy painting an obscene picture of us. Most of the churches didn't know what to do so they stayed silent. People everywhere were being faced with the truth about abortion. A fire was being lit and a light was starting to shine in the darkness.

It was then that rescue became a major national event. We would all converge in one city to focus on the killing that was going on there. There would always be enough of us to sit in front of several killing centers. We were effective; babies were being saved, women helped and Truth sat on the sidewalk with us. Of course it became harder and the non-violent contract we always signed became a real thing. It started to really cost something to rescue; we had to ask ourselves if we were still willing to pay the price.

It was in 1988 that we started to do jail time. Usually it was only a few days. I once went to jail for ten days for playing a pre-born baby's heartbeat on my cassette player, on a public sidewalk. The time we all spent in jail was always productive because the men and women we met there received the message of love and forgiveness through the Gospel of Jesus that we were able to give them.

Then came the time where I spent more than a few days in jail: Atlanta, in August of 1988, I was in three different jails for a period of twenty-one days. We rescued in front of an abortion center that specializes in late term abortions. By late term I mean up to nine months. It is legal to kill your baby up to the moment of birth! There were so many of us that I was actually sitting on the public sidewalk. While the police officer was dragging me away I was pleading with a mom who was at least seven months pregnant not to go in. My heart was crushed for that mother and child. I still can see her face.

At this rescue we chose to do something different. We decided to go as baby John or Jane Doe. Why? To identify with the babies. They never receive a name here on earth and surely do not have any rights! We chose to be their voice, to "sit" in the gap for them and their moms. We hoped that this would wake up America and the killing would stop. We prayed that people would realize that our future was being killed, one by one.

After our arrests, fifty-nine of us were taken to the detention center in downtown Atlanta. Our spirits were filled with the love of Jesus. We sang, prayed and fellowshipped together for the eleven hours we were there. After that we were taken to the city jail. Fellow pro-lifers were already there and they were happy to see us.

The females were segregated from the mainstream inmates for a short time, the males were not. The ladies were put into what looked like a storage room. It was filthy, with lots of bugs and spiders. We had broken cots to sleep on, dirty sheets, no windows, and very stuffy conditions, yet we considered it an honor to be there for our Lord and His children.

The praise and worship to our King was indescribable. The prayers were intense, the fellowship uplifting. Jesus' love and grace washed over us in a really special way. The cots and the food were not fit for human beings. Yet I felt healthy and slept great!

One morning, while still in the storage room, we decided to share Communion. Someone had a box of juice and someone else had some corn chips. On our knees in humble repentance, we worshipped His Majesty and shared our unique Communion, the remembrance of our Lord's sacrifice for us in His body and blood. It was, and still is, the most beautiful time of Communion I've ever experienced.

A few days later we had to go to court for our arraignment. When we arrived at the courthouse, we were put into very large cells that were very old and had not been used in many, many years. There was a very heavy spirit of oppression there, yet in a short time we turned it around for Jesus!

While waiting to go into the court room we began to sing praises to our Lord. Soon, outside where we were being held, a crowd gathered. They could hear our singing and began singing and clapping with us. I know lives were touched deeply that day.

After court we went back to the detention center to wait for the paddy wagon to take us back to the city jail. While there we had the opportunity to talk with a large group of pro-life men who were also waiting for transfer. Several of the men were pastors; they were all being miserably mistreated. They had no showers and no toothbrushes. They slept on the floor, didn't get much food, had no contact with anyone on the outside, and were put in with hard core criminals. The guards really thought they would break these men and they would identify themselves. But God! His mercy and love filled our brothers with His Holy Spirit and over twenty of the inmates accepted Jesus Christ as Lord! Our brothers in Christ were strong and determined. They were an inspiration to us.

Our encounter with our brothers in the Lord was a God-timed thing. After we arrived back at the city jail, we too were mainstreamed. This was done, of course, to scare us and intimidate us to give our names. Jesus quickly turned that around. We didn't miss an opportunity to witness the love of Jesus to the women. We prayed together out loud and many of the inmates joined us. It was powerful, effective and productive to be mainstreamed, and we were grateful.

One lady we met named Mary was eight months pregnant and very sick. We had the opportunity to tell her how much Jesus loves her and her baby. Then we prayed with her for healing and deliverance from drugs. Two days later Mary was transferred to another facility. Later we found out that Mary had full-blown AIDS. Thank You, Jesus, for getting us out of the "storage room" before Mary left!

During this time in jail, the Lord gave us many miracles. All medication had been taken away. It would only be given back if we would tell our names. One lady was on medication for high blood pressure, one for a hormone imbalance and another was taking insulin. The Lord kept them all in good health for the whole time. We were given one uniform, dirty sheets and one blanket. We were not given a pillow, shampoo or any bed clothes. They did give us a little soap, but the showers we were allowed were few and far between; yet, God allowed us to stay clean! The food was deplorable, yet we were not hungry! Was it hard? Yes! God was shining us up with the polishing cloth of sacrifice.

We all were eventually transferred over to the county jail. For this transfer we were separated and I arrived at the county jail with five women I had never met and who were not pro-lifers. We walked into what, I learned later, was called *the pit*. As the large steel door slammed shut with a resounding bang that echoed in my soul, a fear gripped me. All my life I have been afraid of small places and this place was small, hot and stuffy. It was a locked steel pit for sure. My heart was pounding, my stomach churning; I was in a full body sweat. "Lord," I prayed, "please help me. I am here to serve You, take this fear from me." I was calm instantly, and just the sight of me before and after was a witness to the women I was with. We were there for four hours and during that time, one woman recommitted her life to Christ and two others accepted Jesus into their hearts. What was really special is those two ladies ended up being with the pro-lifers and were able to be discipled.

Being processed through the system was a very humiliating experience. One Christian lady refused to be strip searched. A strip search is where you have to take all your clothes off and bend over. She had been molested as a child and would not do it. For this she was beaten severely. When I arrived at the "dorm" where we all stayed, she was lying on her bed badly bruised, but her spirit was strong.

The dorm was a huge room filled with cots, women and lots of noise. The pro-lifers that were there welcomed me warmly and showed me my little space. I was issued two grimy uniforms, two gray sheets, new underwear, thankfully, and a small amount of toiletries. The air conditioner was on full blast during my entire time there and I was constantly cold.

The prison guards were determined to humiliate us as much as possible. They mocked us constantly for our willingness to go to jail to stop abortion. The toilets and the showers were out in the open for all to see, including the male guards. There were no shower curtains, no privacy, and the lights were always brightly shining. We learned to sleep with wash cloths over our eyes and to wash our clothes with hand soap and dry them under our cots. This was a maximum security jail and there were hard core women in with us.

Yet, through it all, the Lord was ever with us. Not once was anything stolen from us. Not once did we feel fear about being with women who were charged with some really serious crimes. Miraculously, we were allowed to pray, sing and read our Bibles. Every morning in the dining room, which was as loud, bright and hectic as our dorm, we sat together, prayed and sang songs to our Lord.

At first only a few women joined us, but soon many of them gathered around. The guards did not stop this because it brought peace to the jail. We learned that if a woman was incarcerated pregnant, the system put a lot of pressure on her to abort the baby. It is less costly to abort than it is to have the women go to term. Needless to say, many babies were saved during this mission trip to jail!

One lady in particular, whose name was Fifi, had been arrested for assault after her boyfriend pressed charges. Five days later the charges were dropped. The only problem was by that time the system had lost her paper work. This lady was extremely ignorant. She was not stupid or dumb, just really uneducated. She was unloved and uncared for throughout her whole life. Fifi had no idea that she was supposed to be arraigned and had a right to have visitors. Basically, the system was treating her the same way she had been treated "outside."

When we arrived there, Fifi was already five months pregnant and had been in there for 100 days! The only thing the jailers had done for her was schedule an abortion. They had told her that she had an abdominal rupture and had to abort her baby.

We counseled her, shared the gospel and led her to Christ. Immediately, via phone calls, we got in contact with the pro-life lawyers. The abortion was stopped and an immediate release was arranged.

The morning Fifi left, at breakfast, she stood up and sang the most beautiful rendition of "He Lives" that I have ever heard. We had arranged for her to receive help once released and I know that she is all right.

Twenty-one days later it was over. A new group of pro-lifers were coming in and we could go home. Much was accomplished for His glory. A song that is very dear to pro-lifers is "Paul & Silas," and we sang it often. Many times we wrote our own verses and one of them went like this:

"God will ask you when you die,
Were you faithful, did you try?"
Yes Lord, we did!

Then came New York City, 1989, and the tombs. Again we were arrested for sitting on the sidewalk. A group of us was taken to the jail in this city called *the tombs*. I believe it was named that because it was very old, run down, overrun with mice and cockroaches and very dirty.

When we first arrived there, sixty of us were put into one cell. It was very crowded and we could not move very much. We were not fed, nor given anything to drink, for the fifteen hours we were there. We sang and prayed and then the Lord gave us a miracle: one of us had a small apple. We prayed over it and all sixty of us had a decent-sized bite of it! Talk about increasing the fish and loaves. We truly serve a wonderful Lord!

Eleven of us were taken out of this cell and were transferred to a much smaller one. It was very dirty, cockroaches were on the walls, mice were seen everywhere and the toilet did not work. It was very cold and none of us ever took our coats off.

I always had my Bible with me and we were really grateful for that. We all were greatly comforted by His Word to us. During the four days that we were there, we were fed twice. Both times were in the middle of the night. We were given one slice of bologna, stale white bread and a small cup of warm Kool-Aid. We were never let out of the cell and we wore the same clothes we came in with. There wasn't any water so we couldn't wash up, brush our teeth or comb our hair. We sure were a sight to see!

Through it all the Holy Spirit comforted us and gave us His compassion for the guards; we witnessed to them about His love. We spent much time interceding for the little ones and their parents.

It is times like these when Scriptures of His Holy Word, such as the following two, burn brightly in our hearts:

"...indeed we share in His sufferings in order that we may also share in His glory." (Romans 8:17)

"But if you suffer for doing good and you endure it, this is commendable before God. To this you were called, because Christ suffered for you, leaving you an example that you should follow in His steps." (1 Peter 2:20b-21)

We knew what we were going through was absolutely nothing compared to what our Lord did for us on the Good Friday so long ago!

One last testimony about this time is very special. For three days we thought that we were alone in this jail. We couldn't hear anyone else. Then on the third night, we heard men singing, "We Shall Overcome," and we knew they were pro-lifers. We started singing back to them. The Holy Spirit's presence was strong and true. It was an awesome experience.

After four days we all were released with our time served.

It was now December of 1989 and Bonnie, a fellow sidewalk counselor, and I had been found guilty of criminal trespass. What we had done is this: we went down the alley driveway of a local abortion center, after receiving permission to do so by a Lieutenant of the nearby police precinct. But, as the way it usually went for us, the Lieutenant denied giving us permission and we were convicted of criminally trespassing.

The day we were to go to court for our sentencing, Bonnie and I went to this abortion center to, again, offer help to the mothers in crisis. That day, each of us had the opportunity to change a mom's mind and get them help. It was a glorious morning!

When we arrived at court for our sentencing, we had no idea that they would take us away immediately. The judge was very pro-abortion and after a few nasty comments such as, "you showed no remorse for your crime," we were handcuffed and dragged away to jail.

We spent that night at the holding tank as we awaited our transfer to the county jail. The time spent there was productive as one of the women we witnessed to was pregnant and planning to abort as soon as she got out. After much conversation this lady accepted Jesus as her Savior and promised not to take her baby's life.

The next morning we were transferred to the county jail. That began, for me, a five month stay on the mission field. The warden immediately made me a trustee and I was given the job of cleaning the front offices along with the wardens. What a blessing that was. Everything I cleaned got prayed over! The Lord gave me many opportunities to witness to the administration of that facility. Let me tell you that a happy face goes a long way in beating back oppression.

Quickly, Bonnie and I began establishing relationships with the other inmates. So much hurt, so much tragedy; "My father raped me when I was twelve and since then I don't care about anything." "I had my first abortion when I was fourteen and I know God hates me…." "I've been on the streets since I was fifteen no one cares about me…." Those were just a few of the comments we listened to just in the first week. The drug withdrawals were very heartbreaking to witness. The pain and suffering that a person goes through from withdrawing from cocaine, heroin or methadone is excruciating. None of the women were given any type of medication to ease the misery of it. They just had to go cold turkey in their cell alone. Needless to say, we were on our knees a lot for these women.

Soon we had a prayer group gathering every evening and many of the women came to know Jesus Christ as their Lord and Savior. So many of these women just needed to know someone cared about them. It is tragic how few of the women had actually heard the Gospel. While in jail I wrote a letter to a fellow Christian. Here is an excerpt of it:

People, we must unite like never before. We cannot effectively witness the salvation message if innocent babies are being slaughtered and we do nothing! If men and women are being destroyed either emotionally or physically by the evil addictions of the world and we do nothing. If the hungry are not fed and we over-eat, if the homeless freeze in our doorways while our heat is turned up, if the thirsty cry for water and we waste our drink, if the prisoner sits alone while we stay at home, and the sick go unattended while we soak our feet. Our witness is an empty vacuum or a barren desert where no seed can take root.

Over and over in Scriptures our Lord tells us: "By our actions… Faith without works is dead…." How can we witness the love of Jesus our Lord with a dead faith? We must become the body of Christ, knitted together with one mind: His! Shouldn't we defend and protect the "least and the littlest" of our fellow human beings? Isn't that a very important part of our belief system? If our hearts do not break for the baby that is literally being torn apart, in a country where we do have the power to stop it then I ask how will we stand for Christ when the hard times come?

This letter did motivate some people to action but I am sad to say, not many.

The majority of women we met in jail had an abortion in their teen years. Most them were sure the Lord would never forgive them. Most of them were led into a life of drugs or prostitution because of shame and guilt. Doesn't that alone tell us something?

After a few weeks we had a productive Bible study going on every evening. This was exciting because we had led many of the women to Christ and were now able to give them a firm Biblical foundation to keep them strong when they got out.

I met a young lady who was about twenty-five years old. She was four months pregnant and would deliver in jail because of the length of her sentence. The medical staff had convinced her to abort. I did have the opportunity to share with her the truth about abortion and how much Jesus loved her. Together we went to the medical staff and cancelled her appointment for the abortion. They were not happy about it at all but could not force her with me there.

Three days later I was taken out to appear in court. When a person is taken out of jail for this reason, they usually have to stay overnight in the holding center. Therefore, I did not get back for a day and a half.

During that time, under extreme pressure, Lilly had the abortion. They were determined to kill this baby and just waited until I was not there. When I saw her, she was sick and shaking. Emotionally distraught, she thought I would hate her for having the abortion. Lilly, with tears flowing, got down on her knees in front of me and asked if I would ever forgive her. Immediately, I was on my knees holding her in my arms and telling her how much Jesus and I love her. You're not suppose to have physical contact but I believe the Lord put a invisible curtain around us and the guard did not see us. How I pray that Lilly is saved and healed. "God, forgive us for what we do."

Sometimes there is victory and sometimes there is not. Sometimes by our witness we can bring a fellow human being into "His green pastures," save babies and minister to broken souls and shattered lives. And sometimes we can just love, be a friend and plant seeds.

During this season of my life, I learned that hope is the bridge on which we walk. Faith is the motivation in us and before us. And love is the light that shines on that bridge!

The Lord accomplished much during this mission trip. Medical care for the pregnant women improved, the Bible study we started continued for years, many guards' hearts were softened and many women were brought to the Lord. Real conversions happened; it wasn't just "jailhouse Jesus." Sure, there were some women who said they accepted Jesus just to be a part of the group, but for a lot of them it was real. There were healings, there were deliverances. Yes, there were dark times and hard times; but in the end, there was a deeper maturity in me, along with a deeper love for the Lord and my fellow human beings.

The following is a testimony from a Christian nurse who worked in the prison system:

In the fall of 1991, I took a position at the holding center in my home town. They had done an F.B.I. investigation on my background and knew of my pro-life activities. During my initial interview we spoke candidly regarding my pro-life beliefs. I was assured then that I would be able to counsel female inmates who were pregnant. I would be allowed to inform them of the alternatives that were available. I was pleased with the dialogue I had with this administration and was looking forward to the opportunities I would have to speak to the female inmates.

Several weeks after I began working there, I found out about a female prisoner that was four to five months pregnant and was scheduled for an abortion the next day. At that time I was working the night shift and had easy access to this lady. I went to her with a fetal model of an in-uterine baby and we spoke for quite a while. She was very upset and did not know what she was going to do. I promised her that I would come back before my shift was over with more information and I spent the night praying for her. I went to my boss and asked if I could bring the information I had regarding alternatives to this lady. He looked it all over and said, "Yes." I went to give her the literature about 5:30 in the morning, just before leaving for the day. The female warden intercepted me and took all the information, telling me she would deliver this information herself.

She did not. Instead, she turned it over to the head supervisor and wrote a report on me. I was accused of harassing the inmate. Then I was told that I could not counsel any of the inmates and that they now had counselors that were assigned to take this responsibility. In other words, the policy had changed in just the few weeks I had been there. I was never informed of the change; instead, I was written up for something that I was told I was allowed to do!

The woman I had talked to did go for the abortion. I was then informed that my counseling her about the truth regarding abortion and telling her she didn't have to do it was totally unacceptable. On the same day, this inmate was complaining about severe stomach cramps and, because I was the nurse on duty, I had to go and evaluate her condition. In seeing the discomfort she was in, I called the hospital where the abortion had taken place. They were very rude to me on the phone and acted like I didn't know what I was doing. Then the head nurse became very upset that I had gone to check on this inmate and told me not to go near her again.

I ended up in Head Nurses office the next day. I was accused of trying to stop the abortion. My reply was that I had been told that I could counsel pregnant inmates regarding alternatives. After being told rudely that I could not do this, I informed them that I could no longer work there and walked out. I found out later that they were going to terminate me anyway. Even though I no longer worked at this holding center I did send this inmate post abortion information and the salvation message." – Sherrie

Isn't the death ethic in this country astounding? The only thing that seems to matter is the amount of money that can be saved by aborting a child as opposed to completing the pregnancy!

Federal Prison Camp

In the previous chapter I wrote a little about my experience in Federal Court.

After many false allegations I was found guilty and sentenced to three months at a federal prison camp. Well, on February 20th of 1996, I surrendered to the Federal Bureau of Prisons at a prison camp over 300 miles away from home. I was to serve ninety days for violating the Federal injunction that now has been proven to be unconstitutional. In other words, I spent ninety days in a prison camp for something I now have the right to do!

Does this upset me? Absolutely not! I truly believe that each time a pro-lifer went to jail for standing up for life the Lord worked through us. Much was always accomplished in all the incarcerations.

> *His Holy Word tells us: "My grace is sufficient for you, for My power is made perfect in weakness." (2 Corinthians 12:9a)*

Perfect means complete and mature. *Weakness* means to lack strength and *grace* means divine influence upon the heart and its reflection in our lives.

When I entered the prison camp, I became weak. I did not have the strength on my own to control any part of my life. It now belonged to the prison camp. In the first week I tried on my own to be strong and failed miserably. It was then I gave myself fully into

His hands. And His grace was (is, and always will be) truly more than sufficient. In my weakness as the only pro-life prisoner there, far away from family and friends, His power was made mature in me. For the rest of my time at this camp I was at peace, rejoicing in His love and motivated to action by His Holy Spirit. With His peace and guidance I was able to accomplish the chores that the Lord had planned for me to do.

I met women there who had been in the system for many years and had many more years to go. These women had met Jesus while in and had become strong in faith. They had truly repented of their crimes and had let go of any bitterness that they had once had. They were Christians who were kind, compassionate and sensitive. They humbled me because when I began to talk to them I wondered how I would be maintaining my faith after being in prison for five or ten years. One woman had been incarcerated for almost twenty! The reason she was at the camp was because of her good behavior. She had committed murder over twenty years ago and had completely changed. I wondered how I would be, living under the stress of that camp for years? Having to be with the same people twenty-four hours a day, seven days a week? Wearing the same prison uniform month after month, year after year? How strong would I stay in dealing with the abusive attitudes of the guard constantly? Would I have the same attitude that they had toward the Lord, toward life itself? Meeting these women caused me to really pray daily for strong faith. I learned a lot about myself, and about enduring faith through the women I met there.

Of course I met women who were hard core, and cared about nothing. Women who were not sorry for their crimes, only that they had been caught. Women who were close-minded and unwilling to listen. Then there were the women who were open to the Gospel and ready to get saved!

Even though I was trying to be strong in my own strength, the Lord was gently leading me into His arms. The first night I was at the camp I was standing outside the cafeteria with fellow inmates. Suddenly I heard voices and guitars praising the Lord. At first I thought, "The Lord is letting me hear His angels to comfort me." However, after a minute I knew it was actual people singing and I asked the lady that I was standing next to what was going on. She told me that it was Wednesday night fellowship and I could go and join them if I wanted to. If I wanted to!! I was inside in a flash. What a comfort to my spirit and what a joy to my soul. Every Wednesday from that one until I was released I attended this fellowship.

In the prison camp there was a lot of upheaval and confusion. They changed the "rules of the day" every day. Sometimes the rules in the afternoon were different from the morning. Yet it was our responsibility to know and obey them all. If we didn't, we were sent "down the hill" to the maximum security prison located there. There, one would be put into what was called segregation. This was a small cell apart from all others in the dark with one light hanging from the ceiling. It was dirty with no running water; not a nice place at all. Depending on the infraction, you could be there for days or months; isolated from everyone and everything except the guard who brought the food.

It was like standing under a large steel ball and if you moved the wrong way it would drop and crush you; that was how intense the stress level was all the time. There aren't any locks or prison walls; yet, the rules, the emotional abuse and the disrespect was just as confining. Remember, I had already been in maximum and minimum security jails so I did have some experiences to compare it to.

At this camp an inmate is free to see what it was like to be free. Let me explain: we were allowed to go outside, yet only so far. We could walk, yet only in certain areas. Stepping one foot off the designated area meant a breach of the rules. In my experience in the jail mission field, this time was the most emotionally and mentally draining by far.

There weren't any clocks in the main area. The only clock was in the educational room and that was very far out of the way to get to. A strange thing happens to a person when they never know what time it is. However, we had to be on time for all assignments and appointments or else we broke the rules. Sounds impossible, doesn't it? Well, an inmate *is* allowed to have a watch sent in or purchase one at an outrageous price. There is a prison store which is called the Commissary. I'll explain that a little later. It took six weeks for me to have a watch sent in and until then all I did was ask anyone who had a watch what time it was. We would be told to be at "medical" at a certain time and if we were one minute late we would be written up. Somehow, we were sure to be on time. Upon arrival at a given appointment we would sign in and then wait hours to be seen.

There are four counts in a twenty-four hour period. A count is where an inmate had to be standing next to their bed to be counted. Two of the counts occurred at 4:00pm and at 9:30 pm and the others at various times in the middle of the night. The 4:00 and 9:30 count was National, meaning all Federal Prisons in the country would do this count at the same time and it would go into the main computer. During these counts we had to be in our "cube" at attention, standing next to our bunks, no talking or movement. It was always a tense time because if we moved or made a sound it was automatic segregation.

I tell you that to tell you this: at one of the four o'clock counts about two months into my sentence there was more than the usual tension. The guards even seemed to be nervous. We knew something was very wrong. The count was finished, which usually took about twenty minutes. There were 220 women in this camp which was built to hold 90!

The administrator came on the loud speaker and said, "The count is not cleared, stay where you are." Meanwhile, the inmates whose cubes were by the windows indicated the guards were surrounding the camp and they were armed. We assumed someone had tried to escape. Then suddenly there was a flurry of movement. Over twenty-five women were dragged from their cubes, lined up in the hall and surrounded by the guards. They were not allowed to get dressed (some were in their bathrobes as they were preparing to take a shower after the count). They could not put their shoes on or take any of their belongings. All of these women were marched out and down the hill to the maximum security prison!

It was horrible, and very reminiscent of Nazi Germany. We found out later that Mr. Clinton had signed a bill deporting any immigrants who were in prison in this country. This was all done without a hearing or due process of law. Several of these women were from Cuba and we knew they would be executed when they arrived back in Cuba. We also found out later that the women taken were not fed that night and were not given bedding, or even a bed, to sleep on. They were treated worse than animals. It was one of the most heart-wrenching experiences I've ever had.

I understand that our attitudes have changed since 9/11 and the need for greater security and scrutiny is absolutely necessary. But this was 1996, and all these women had non-violent convictions. Not one of them were political, violent or against our society. There wasn't a good reason for this type of treatment.

The count at night was usually done with a flash light waving in your face. If you were in the bathroom, the male guards had no problem walking in and checking. This included time of taking showers. There was absolutely no dignity. I was only there for three months. Just think about the women that are there for years!

I was in a cube in the basement of the building. A cube is 7 x 7 feet with two bunks, two steel lockers and that was it. The guards were always looking for "contraband." Contraband was anything on their list that should not be in our lockers such as gum, salt, sugar or basically anything they decided to call contraband. One inmate was sent to segregation for two weeks for having an open box of juice in her locker. They accused her of trying to make liquor. This was ridiculous because the juice they found would not turn into alcohol. Everything depended on the mood of the administration and how they felt about you that day. I sometimes feel like we were rats in a maze and they were experimenting with our minds to see how far they could go.

The medical treatment was deplorable. One lady broke her foot in a fall. They refused to x-ray her foot for three weeks. Finally, when they did, they discovered the foot was broken. Then they set it all wrong. She will be a cripple for the rest of her life. Remember, this was a low security prison camp for non-violent, white-collared crimes. I became very close to a lady who was sixty-five years old at the time. As a matter of fact, we worked together in the laundry. She was very special to me and we had many great hours of fellowship.

When I first met her she swore a lot but after a while and a lot of witnessing she was praising the Lord instead. I tried very hard to care for her as she was not well and had a lot of physical problems. Every time she would go to medical to get some relief they would ignore her complaints. One time she was in a tremendous amount of pain and went to see the so-called doctor. They became very angry at her for being there again and body slammed her against the wall.

We called her daughter. She called the administration but to no avail. We sure did a lot of praying. Once I laid my hands on her and asked the Lord to heal her. For a long time she did feel much better. I was with her for her sixty-sixth birthday and we had a neat little surprise party for her.

After I got out I stayed in contact with a lot of the inmates and they told me that as soon as I was released she became very sick. They finally sent her to the prison hospital in Texas. My dear sister was riddled with cancer. They refused to give her any treatment; they said she was too far gone. Yet they would not release her to die with her family around her. In the end, my friend died in a prison hospital, all alone. I talked with her daughter afterwards and found out that her family was not allowed to be with her in the end. This woman had been sentenced to four years for drug conspiracy; a non-violent crime. She should have been allowed to die surrounded by those who loved her.

I do praise the Lord with all my heart that I had the opportunity to introduce her to a personal relationship with Jesus, our Savior. I look forward to the day when I shall see her again in heaven.

When you are with people for twenty-four hours a day, seven days a week, you get to know them pretty well. One lady was a trained and licensed medical professional. One of her patients, during a therapy session, told her of a crime he had committed. She refused to tell the Feds what this man had told her during the session. It was an issue of patient confidentiality. She was charged with conspiracy, convicted and sent to the camp for eighteen months. This was an honorable woman who refused to break her vows no matter what it cost her.

Just before I arrived at the camp she had become violently ill with food poisoning. The medical staff refused to treat her. Four days later, dehydrated and weak, she passed out in the bathroom. Finally, they sent her to the prison hospital down the hill. After hydrating her, they told her to go back up to the camp. The guards refused to drive her up the hill. So, in the middle of the cold winter night, this lady had to walk up the hill with only her nightgown and slippers on. This is a walk that usually takes ten minutes; it took her over half an hour to make it up. She wouldn't talk, and there was a price to pay!

The camp had a shrink and every woman had to go see him. My time with him was very uneventful and he really didn't want to talk to me. He was very self-centered and cared nothing for the women. He would even tell them they were hopeless, and deliberately try to hurt them. Many times I ended up praying with a woman who had just seen him.

It's ok to laugh when you're crying.

What is *loneliness*? It is the emptiness of the heart. I see the women laughing, talking, staying busy with crafts or jobs but when I look into their eyes, I see the loneliness, the longing for freedom and family that burns strongly from within. We surround ourselves with people and things to do but nothing ever satisfies the loneliness, nothing except the love Jesus offers freely. A smile, a word of encouragement or a gift from the commissary can make all the difference in the world. As ambassadors for Christ, that's our purpose; to give His love away. We are to let the lost know they don't have to be lonely and that our Lord is waiting to comfort and strengthen.

Then one Sunday during a church service, as so many of the women were going forward to accept Jesus as their Lord and Savior, the Lord put it on my heart to do some type of follow up. The Chaplin was overworked; therefore, there wasn't a discipleship program for the new Christians.

I called home and asked for new Bibles to be sent in. Praise the Lord: over two hundred were sent within a week. The Chaplin gave me permission to write a simple "Now What?" paper to be inserted in the Bibles. They were then given to the new converts. I cannot tell you how much the women appreciated receiving a Bible of their own.

The following week I was asked to start a weekly Bible study. The way the Lord Jesus opens doors for His work never ceases to amaze me. Grateful and excited, I put together a simple six-week course. It went very well, and when I left I gave all the lessons to a mature lady in the Lord. She promised to continue teaching the new converts His ways and to give them His comfort.

While I was at the camp, many of my brothers and sisters in the Lord sent me financial support. Many of the incarcerated women are not supported by anyone on the outside. The need is great. We need to purchase everything from laundry soap to stamps to mail our letters. All the women had a job at the camp, we were paid twelve cents an hour and at the end of the month that really didn't add up to very much. So what I would do with the money sent to me is purchase what was needed by my fellow inmates. When they would try to pay me back I would tell them, "Pass it on. Buy something for someone else who has a need." It was a wonderful opportunity to bless others, teach a lesson in giving and display faith in action. All this because of the generosity of fellow believers!

Throughout the whole time I was at the prison camp, I could feel the prayers from fellow believers. Every time my heart would begin to sink, their prayers would lift me up again. The letters I received were extremely important as well. They made my heart sing. It was the hand of freedom reaching in, touching and strengthening me.

During this mission trip I learned some very meaningful lessons. When I first arrived, I was told by a fellow inmate, "Don't let the time do you, you do the time." Those words taught me a great lesson that I apply even to my freedom. Too often we let events and times dictate our lives when the reality is that God created time for us to move forward in! Time is ours to use, not belong to. That principle was of great benefit to me during the months that I was incarcerated. It still is.

Another powerful lesson was the truth that our actions speak louder than our words. We can talk the talk but unless we walk the walk our words are clanging cymbals making useless noise. It was faith in action that moved the women to fall in love with Jesus.

One miraculous event that I will never forget occurred just before my release: My daughter was expecting her fourth child and I had crocheted a little afghan for my new grandchild. One morning I took the afghan to the laundry with me to wash it and prepare it for packing. I went to lunch and when I got back, the afghan was gone; someone had stolen it.

My first reaction was one of anger. Everyone heard and saw how angry I was. I was very vocal and very upset. Then the Lord spoke to my heart about forgiveness and my heart became filled with sorrow for my actions. Yes, the afghan was very special, but I could always make another one. With a humble and contrite heart, I publicly apologized for my attitude and actions. I made it clear that I forgave whoever took it and that I would make another one. In less than two hours, the afghan was amazingly found! What a lesson I learned that day. Forgiveness and love in action; that's what the Lord wants from us.

I spent Easter, Mother's day and my wedding anniversary in prison. Because of those times, another profound lesson was learned. Especially at Easter time. When Holy Week approached I began to become really depressed. My family is very close and we do many traditional things during this special week. I was missing it all and was not very happy about it.

Once again, the Lord taught me about His love. The Lord of all, the Creator of the Universe, loved us so much that He walked with us, taught us and then suffered pain to a degree that we will never be able to comprehend. He left his home in heaven and became "...despised and rejected by men, a man of sorrows, and familiar with suffering" (Isaiah 53: 3a) and *I* should be depressed?! I got on my face before our wonderful Savior and again asked for forgiveness. I prayed that He would use me to comfort others during this special time. I had many other years to spend with my family and some of the other women didn't even have families. Furthermore, many of the ones who did have families had been rejected by them. It ended up being a very special Easter. I smiled a lot that wonderful Sunday!

I am not alone in the awesome events experienced in prison. Other Christians who have gone to jail for Jesus express, over and over, how the time they did caused their faith to deepen and mature. All of us have learned about real humility, about a real thankfulness for life and a deeper understanding of the love Jesus has for all of humanity.

Pastor Mark shares his testimony with us:

Just a few years prior to my prison experience in Atlanta, Georgia, I had accepted Jesus Christ as my

Lord and Savior. I was still in the process of learning to understand salvation and what it meant to me. I was learning that I had to exercise my faith in daily action.

Then I had the opportunity to go to Atlanta to truly put action to my faith in the battle for life. I was both excited and anxious to put action to my pro-life rhetoric. When we arrived I could feel the strong presence of the Holy Spirit.

I witnessed first-hand how our country was polarized by the holocaust of abortion. It was then that I realized I would have to be willing to lay my life down for those who were being carried to their death. Now I was beginning to understand the Biblical principle involved in Christians standing (sitting) in the gap for the innocent babies who had no way to defend or speak for themselves.

In humility and repentance I went to the line, along with many others, and sat down in front of an abortion center. We were in a peaceful, humble position and the Lord truly ministered to our hearts. What a marvel it was for me to really experience the lesson of trusting the Lord. As I sat down I could feel His grace come upon me. When we really are willing to lay our lives down for Him, He truly fills us with His strength, His comfort and His peace. His love and grace supersedes any fear or doubt we may have.

We sang songs of praise and worship. We prayed in humble repentance for our Lord to stop the killing. As I sat there I remembered that God didn't treat me the way I should be treated, but with mercy and forgiveness. I prayed that day that God would treat our sinful country with the same mercy and forgiveness.

One by one we were arrested. It was very difficult as the police were extremely rough. I could see excruciating pain on the faces of my fellow rescuers. As they approached me, the grace of the Holy Spirit totally filled me. Fear was gone and His peace was with me. I cannot recall any pain or even how I was carried away.

On the way to jail, we were all calling out the window of the bus to the people of Atlanta to repent and stop killing in their city. We then were put into jail and it was one of the most incredible experiences of my life. I was in jail for eight days with 240 other men. Forty of us were pastors.

We had three services a day and during these services I listened to some of the most inspired teachings that I have ever heard in my life. The worship was anointed.

We gathered in a big open area and together we would kneel in worship of our Lord. The supernatural impact was miraculous! I witnessed first hand; men healed, baptized in the showers, sheets were multiplied (the men had not been given enough sheets for everyone to have one) and lives being completely transformed. My heart was forever changed by the love Jesus was pouring out.

Salvation was no longer a thought, or a belief system, it had now become a way of life! The Scripture: "In the same way, faith by itself, if it is not accompanied by action, is dead." (James 2:17) became very clear in my mind and actions.

I was happy to get out yet at the same time I will cherish the moments I experienced while I was in jail for Jesus.

I would like to add just a little to this testimony because Pastor Mark is my son and I witnessed his arrest in Atlanta.

That day, my daughter, my pastor and my son were rescuing at the local abortion center in Atlanta. My daughter is very petite and the police just picked her up and carried her away. Her experience in jail was as awesome as my son Mark's. However, both my pastor and my son are big men and the police used unnecessary force to move them.

First, I saw the pain they were inflicting upon my pastor by the neck-hold they were using. By this time I was on my knees weeping from the bottom of my heart. I was witnessing brutality on gentle, non-violent Christians for no reason, except to inflict pain.

Then it was my son the police were standing over. I have often thought about the heartbreak Mary must have felt as she watched her Son suffer. Witnessing the pain and suffering of someone who is a part of you; someone you love with all your heart, and knowing it has to be. In watching what they did to mine I received just the smallest taste of her suffering.

When I saw the police grab my son in such a way that I thought they were breaking his shoulders, I wanted to run over to him and exchange places. I wanted to stop it with every fiber of my being. Yet the Lord, in His mercy, kept me on my knees. It was something that He had given Mark to do and I could not take his blessings from him. In finding out what a blessing it did turn out to be, I thank Jesus I obeyed Him.

There is not one Christian that I have ever met in the pro-life ministry that regrets going to jail for Jesus and His babies. Every one of them has a powerful testimony of opportunities the Lord gave them to minister His love. All have learned to have a deeper walk with our Lord and Savior!

The following is a powerful testimony from Pastor Mike:

"But God's Word is not chained." (2 Timothy 2:9b)

On December 11th, in a city court, the judge sent Mary Beth, a married woman with two children, and me to the County Jail. We were sent there without bail or bond, pending our sentencing for a conviction stemming from distributing pamphlets at a hospital where abortions are committed.

The pamphlets exposed the hospital's two abortion clinics and its support of doctor-assisted suicide. After spending five days in jail, I was sentenced to the maximum of ninety days and Mary Beth received thirty days.

While awaiting this sentence the peace and joy of the Lord enveloped us. We were able, by His grace, to give an account to the court of the hope that kept us.

The courtroom was filled with supporters that overflowed into the foyer. The Christians that were outside were singing in worship and the sound wafted into the court room. The sound was like an angelic choir comforting our spirits.

Because of His grace, worry or fret did not overtake us and we were both consumed with concern for the Judges heart in front of our Holy God!

Genesis 50:9 gives an account regarding a man named Joseph. He was sold into slavery by his brothers out of jealousy. This particular Scripture points to the ability of God to turn a seemly hardship into a vehicle to show forth His purpose and power.

The Scripture reads: **"But Joseph said to them, 'Don't be afraid. Am I in the place of God? You intended to harm me, but God intended it for good to accomplish what is now being done, the saving of many lives.'" (Genesis 50:19-20)**

As in the story of Joseph, we saw God do amazing things, saving many inmates from their sins and bringing them to life in Christ. During the first few days we were in an area called "reception." No, there wasn't soft music and snacks. This is an area where prisoners are classified for placement and medical needs.

The women and men are in separate areas, thus Mary Beth and I saw each other infrequently. It was in reception that I met a man named Bruce. Bruce asked me for a glass of water, as I was free to move about and he was in his cell twenty-three hours a day. "Surprised," is an understatement to describe his reaction when I told him I was a pastor.

This information seemed to fire up his determination to open up his heart and declare his need for Christ. In our conversation, Bruce started to recall the stories he had learned from the Bible as a child. Under heavy conviction, Bruce recognized his sin and his need for repentance and change. At the end of our discourse, Bruce received Christ as His Lord and Savior.

And then there was José. José had been a drug kingpin and he was desperate. His little kingdom had imploded and he was under suicide watch. José would say to me as I walked by him, "Why are you hurting me?" I would respond with, "José, the devil wants to hurt you, but Jesus will save you if you open your heart to Him." I would go over to his cell and pray over him. Pray that his heart would open to the Love of Christ that awaits all who ask.

After three days in this area, I got word that I was moving. I still pray for José.

It was off to the Public Safety Building. There, I ran right into another move of God. A brother in the Lord, named Anthony, a large man about three hundred pounds and 6′5″, was compelling men to come to the Bible study he was holding. And they sure were coming! There were about fifteen men, twice a day, attending this Bible study.

This Bible study soon turned into a mini church with two deacons, Lester and Michael. I became the visiting pastor and doors were opened in a tremendous way. In the first two days, there was a season of repentance and rededication in this group.

Two men came to Christ during this time. One of these men had been at the end of his rope. He had lost all; his wife, his business, and his children because of wrong decisions. Jesus, in His mercy, picked this man up and placed life in him. Where there once was nothing but emptiness and death now was filled with hope and love. This man had been sleeping twenty hours a day in a deep depression when Jesus broke through and shattered the chains of sin that held him.

Another young man in trouble, for the first time in his life cried out to Jesus for forgiveness. The saving grace of our Lord was on the move in a powerful way.

A drug addict rededicated his life to Christ and made a promise to go back to the church he had been attending. At that church he had stayed clean for over three years. We truly do need each other. His heart now had the deep desire to be reconciled with his children and begin a new, changed life! A young man, hearing the claims of Christ, opened his heart to the love of God. After five very busy days I was moved, once again.

It was at this jail I was able to see my wife. She looked so good, yet tired and drawn. The Lord was keeping her and my children close to His heart and our brothers and sisters in the Lord were providing for their needs. We only had one hour to be together. An hour can seem so long at times yet this one virtually flew by.

In this new jail, the Lord impressed upon me to start a Bible study. Each evening, at 7:00 P.M., we would gather to break open the Word of God. It was so rich and refreshing. This study made me appreciate the meetings at our church. As the word got around as to why I was there, some of the men began to nick-name me: Pamphlet man, Bible Bob and the Rev.! Even in this teasing the doors would open for witnessing. I often considered how fortunate I was to be in jail in this country, and not China or Cuba, for my faith in Christ. Here, I had three meals a day, hot showers, a warm bed, and visitations from my family and friends. I received regular mail and had phone use. In the other countries, Christians are routinely tortured, deprived and killed for their faith. Visits from loved ones, much less receiving any mail, is virtually unheard of.

As the whirlwind brought us into prison, it blew us out unexpectedly! On December 24th, I was called to appear in court. Our attorney had filed an appeal and much to the chagrin of the D.A. we were released without bail or bond, pending the appeal. As I was packing to leave, the Lord gave me one more indication that He was in control of this whole experience.

Another man, hopeless and bound in sin came to talk to me. He opened his heart regarding the guilt and bondage that sin had worked into him. While the guard was urging me to finish packing to leave, this man broke before a Holy and Loving God and invited Christ into his heart. "Truly Jesus, You do all things well and Your Word is not chained, but powerful and able to deliver man from the clutches of a defeated devil and the power of sin. Thank You for letting me serve You. Amen."

Mary Beth's testimony is just as powerful:

The Lord was so very faithful to me while I was in prison. I give Him all the praise with a grateful heart for all who prayed and helped while I was separated from my family. I was blessed daily by cards, notes and letters. Every time I called home, my husband and daughters would share with me how our church family was helping them in so many different ways. Meals were brought, rides were provided, whatever was needed was there for them. One of my friends went to my home and baked Christmas cookies with my daughters. Another took my girls Christmas shopping. I cannot state how grateful I was for all the support and love given to my family in this time of need.

Our Lord comforted me and worked through me during my time in jail. He provides for us even when we are not aware of it. I saw so many of God's truths being lived out while I was in.

I spent the first three days in jail in a cell isolated from everyone. Jesus was so faithful to me during this time. I had this time to pray for my husband, children, Pastor Mike, his family and all the other faithful pro-lifers incarcerated. Even though I was in the cell alone, I did get to talk to some of the other women through the walls. It was there I met Kathy. She had been clean for one year, was going to church, had gotten baptized and her life had been improving. Until she fell and used drugs one night and tried to break into her boyfriend's home. She had gotten caught and now was awaiting her sentence.

Kathy went before the judge and had gotten one more month in jail. She cried for three hours straight. During this time I began to read to her from the Gospel of John and she began to calm down. I was able to share with her that she needs godly sorrow instead of the worldly sorrow she was now experiencing. We talked of the difference between the two and I know her heart was touched. So many of the women were crying and being upset not because of the wrong they did but because they had gotten caught. They had a very strong tendency of blaming others for the trouble they were in. The Lord was giving me the opportunity to tell them the truth. We only have ourselves to blame, not others and in doing that we are free to accept His forgiveness and love.

My friends Jerry and Terry sent in two New Testaments and a book of Psalms. I gave Kathy a New Testament. She prayed with me and said she finally could see that it was good that she was still in jail. Kathy admitted that the desire to do drugs had become strong in her again and she had planned to use again once she was released. Now, she said, she wanted to stay clean and live for Jesus. She was moved into a different area but came to see me the next day to thank me for praying with her and giving her the little Bible. She felt so much better now and knew with the Lord she could do it right.

Soon the other women learned I was a Christian, in jail because of my stand for life. The other New Testament and book of Psalms quickly was given away and the women began to pass them around for all to read!

When I would have fleeting moments of fear, doubt and worry I would open up my Bible and His Words would give me such comfort. When we are in a situation where we are totally powerless and stripped down to the very basics of life, His Holy Spirit is very strong and we learn about truly leaning on Him for everything! This experience made me truly long for our true hope and that is eternal life with Him. There we will have nothing to distract us from Him and His glorious presence. My prayer was to be even more faithful and focused on Him on the outside. There are so many distractions and unimportant things that I had so often stumbled on and I was beginning to recognize how truly important it was to always focus on my Lord, not on things.

I was finally moved into an area with twenty-six women in one big room with bunk beds. I had been transferred with four other women that I was getting to know and become friends with. I was grateful to know someone because we were not welcomed by some of the other women. Women in jail can be really tough and nasty, it can get really scary. So it was good that the five of us stuck together.

Yet the Lord worked in so many wonderful ways over the next five days. The group of hostile women really had it out for me because they knew why I was there. They did everything they could to try to provoke me so I would argue or fight with them. However the Holy Spirit gave me a strong spirit of self-discipline. One by one they started to soften and began to open their hearts to me. Then two of them started to study Scriptures with me, another few shared their lives with me and asked me to pray for them and with them several times. A few of these women have no one on the outside and I plan on visiting them when released. I learned, after I was released, that many Christians were praying for my protection while I was in. I know that those prayers were answered as not only was I protected but had the opportunity to minister the Love of Jesus to these lost women.

Bonnie, who was one of the four that had transferred with me, accepted Christ just before she was released. Kelly, who was three months pregnant, was thinking about having an abortion. She did not know who the father of her child was and the nurse of the jail was going to take her for the abortion. Kelly had two days to make her decision when I met her. I showed her in Scripture that God knows us even before we are formed in the womb and He has a purpose for every person He creates. She kept going back and forth and finally she said she would keep her child. I was so excited. So many women were pregnant in both the jails that I was in. I thank the Lord that He gave me the opportunity to speak life into my friend Kelly!

Again, I was transferred to another jail. The deputy there was a born again Christian and she put me in a cubical by myself. That night I slept very well. The next day more women were brought in and I had to have a roommate. This lady was a lesbian and I had no idea what to expect.

It was crazy at this jail. It was just like what Ephesians 4:18-19 states: **"They are darkened in their understanding and separated from the life of God because of the ignorance that is in them due to the hardening of their hearts. Having lost all sensitivity, they have given themselves over to sensuality so as to indulge in every kind of impurity with a continual lust for more."** Both of the jails were full of the fruits of the flesh but this one was really bad. That got to me every once in a while. I needed to keep my mind renewed because it would get full of things that did not belong there. For the first few days I did not feel very useful in God's work. When a local Pastor came to see me, I shared my frustration with him. He told me that if the Lord used me in jail He was sovereign and even if He did not use me He was still sovereign. With those words of comfort I learned to just rest in our Lord's presence.

It was then that I was able to minister and confront my roommate and her girlfriend's sin. Monique (my roommate) had grown up in a church and said Jesus would understand because she had been terribly hurt by her husband. I read Scriptures to her showing her she did not have to live in that lifestyle. The Lord gave me favor with both women. They actually liked me and listened to me, even though I was confronting their sin. Monique prayed with me before I left and repented of her sin. I have visited her since I've been released and we did a great Bible study together.

I became encouraged in this dark place when I met a lady named Tina. She had come to Jesus while in jail, before I got there. We would sit and share the Word together and pray for His strength.

Then the morning came when I was called to go back to court. I wondered what more I had done and had no idea why they wanted me back in court. After an hour wait, Pastor Mike and I were called into the court room. There stood our lawyer, John, and he was making an appeal to the judge. Praise the Lord; she agreed to free us, even though the D.A. fought hard against it. Walking out of court, I turned around and looked at John. He smiled and said, "Merry Christmas."

The deputy releasing us said that getting out on an appeal so fast had never happened in this court. He said we must have known the judge. Pastor Mike said, "We do know the Judge!"

There were several people waiting to welcome us to freedom. It was a wonderful feeling to walk out the door of that court house. To see my husband and daughters and know we were all going home together filled me with great joy. How blessed it is to be a part of the body of Christ. I thank the Lord everyday for His love and faithfulness.

What you have read are just a few of the untold stories by the forgotten Christians who willingly laid their lives down to stand up for Christ and His innocent children. You've read about men and women who went to jail and witnessed the love of Jesus to the lost; men who gave comfort to the fathers whose children had been killed by the butcher's knife and women who gave hope to the women who had no hope. Jails were turned into churches for a season. Peace always followed the pro-lifer who went to jail. Even the jailers were happy to see us. They knew we would bring love and hope into such dark places.

We all found it easy to press into the Lord when we went to jail. There is such an intensity of the presence of the Holy Spirit. His Word, in Matthew 25:36b, says, "I was in prison and you came visit me." And visit we did. Our Lord walked with us, directed us, and led us in every move we made. In jail, without any distractions of the world, we learned to lean on Jesus like never before. It truly was a productive mission field of the Living God!

Then we were thrust back into the mainstream of life where another spectrum of emotions and thoughts filled our hearts and minds. During the time we were in jail it was almost a spiritual high and when the time was done, we did come down. We had so many decisions to make and decisions which used to be automatic became more complex. Our family and friends wanted to hear about the experiences but only for a short time. We needed to talk about it more than anyone wanted to listen. There was a strong need to release all we heard, felt, and saw while we were in jail, yet there really wasn't a way to tell it like it really was.

Surprisingly, we missed the people we were in with and we thought we were crazy for missing them.

A profusion of thoughts and feelings constantly cascaded over us as we tried to become "normal" again; however, it never would be the same again. A person just doesn't go to jail for Jesus and not change. For a season I found myself angered that people didn't appreciate all the blessings they had, especially freedom. I found it difficult to pray with the same intensity that I had while in jail. Yet, life went on and the passion renewed itself. I believe what all of us learned in jail is now ingrained in our lives and the Lord uses those experiences to remind us to always have His compassion and love for others.

I believe that I speak for most of the pro-lifers who went to jail for Jesus and life when I say that our relationship with Jesus grew deeper and more mature. The need to press into Him causes all the head knowledge that we have about our Lord and His Word to became a beautiful, living garden growing within our hearts. The Living Bible became living the Bible. The desire to know Him more and serve Him more became the main driving force in our lives.

Our eyes, ears, and hearts have been opened to see what the "dark side" is like. Our hearts are opened and vulnerable to the sorrow the Lord feels for the lost. We saw the desperate need of the poor and oppressed, and we were moved to action. We are humbled because we are saved. We are determined with a new resolve, to share the salvation message with the lost and we never forget.

There are hundreds of testimonies yet unwritten. I know for myself I have not written even half of my experiences in jail. Furthermore, I am sure that all who have contributed to this chapter would say the same. Testimonies of guards saved, judges saved, miracles of healing and deliverance, tragic heartbreak healed, babies saved from the abortionist's knife; all by the sweet love of Jesus that dwells within the believer. Yet enough is written here so that you may know what happened when Christians went to jail in the United States for Christ and Life. Is it worth it? You decide!

Chapter 7

What We Believe

You've met us on the field of victory, the blood-soaked field of heartbreak, with our rainbows and our tears. You've read our words in the courtroom and seen our lives behind prison walls. We have shared our hearts, our purpose, and our innermost beings. We are a peculiar people. We are the forgotten Christians; the unknown soldiers of the Lord.

Thank you for taking the time to read this book. This chapter is dedicated to sharing what we believe. May it move your heart to action. In every city across this country there is some type of pro-life remnant, find it and get involved. The lives of unborn babies count on you!

> ***"...The fate of unborn millions will now depend, under God, on the courage and conduct of this army. Our cruel and unrelenting enemy leaves us only the choice of brave resistance or the most abject submission. We have, therefore, to resolve to conquer or die." George Washington.***

My question here is what ever happened to that resolve in our country?

I truly believe that the sin of abortion is so insidious and so intertwined with the grievous moral decline of our country that if we do not do everything we can to stop it the soul of our country will be lost.

We all talk about the war on terror. We argue about Iraq and Afghanistan and yet we kill 3,300 pre-born babies a day in the United States! Approximately 20,000 murders are committed a year in our country. Why is that never discussed? Furthermore, could someone tell me where logic and common sense went? Because it sure is missing!

The media, in general, has become perverted and one-sided. Kids are killing kids in our schools, and we just continue on our merry blind way. Isn't it time to really wake up, pray up and take action?

One of the times I was in court I was accused of creating my own truth. Why? Because I made the statement that abortion kills human beings. Truth is truth and it is not relative to the moment we are in nor relative to whatever we want it to be relative too. Life is life, and death is dead; that is the truth.

From the moment of conception, a human being is complete in the fact that the entire DNA is there. All that is needed is time and nutrition. That is truth. When the suction machine goes on and a little human being is torn to shreds, a little girl or boy dies. That is truth. Abortionists take their instruments and cut human beings into pieces, remove the legs, arms and head from within a mother, and then put all the parts on the table to make sure all the body is out. A little boy or girl lives no longer. That is truth. The mother and the father are still a mother and father. Now they are the parents of a dead human being. That is truth.

"...Cain attacked his brother Abel and killed him. Then the Lord said to Cain, 'Where is your brother Abel?' 'I don't know,' he replied, 'Am I my brother's keeper?' The Lord said, 'What have you done? Listen! Your brother's blood cries out to me from the ground.'" (Genesis 4:8b-10)

If Abel's blood cried out to God how loud must the cries be of the millions upon millions of dead babies? Furthermore, aren't we supposed to be our brother's keepers?

Yes, much is being done in the pro-life mission field. Crisis pregnancy centers now have sonogram machines and most of them have decent funding. Pro-lifers are using the internet to get the life message out. The Supreme Court has outlawed partial birth abortion. However, the court does not have the means to enforce this ruling; therefore, it is ineffective and partial birth abortion still is committed. The amount of abortion centers has dramatically decreased. Many doctors will no longer commit abortions. Post abortion counseling is now readily available. There have even been very good documentaries on TV regarding the development of the pre-born baby. In 1987, it was 4,400 pre-born babies being killed a day. It has gone down 1,000 since then. Yes, we are being effective to a degree…

So what more can we do to effectively stop the horrible moral decline in our country and stop the evil of killing pre-born babies, the exploitation of mothers and the neglect of the fathers?

Do I think we should go back out and sit in front of our local killing centers, get arrested and go to jail? No, I think that was a season in time. It was to wake us up and let us know just what the truth about abortion was and is. We no longer can say, "We didn't know."

As I am writing this book a movement called the Forty days for Life has begun across our nation. We, as the body of Christ, are starting to get on our knees and repenting on the street in front of our local killing centers obeying the Scripture that states: **"If my people, who are called by my name, will humble themselves and pray and seek my face and turn from their wicked ways, then will I hear from heaven and will forgive their sin and will heal their land." (2 Chronicles 7:14)**

Yet the number of Christians and churches involved is very low. However, it is a start and in that we rejoice!

I am completely convinced that if the Christians would receive the courage that Jesus gives freely, they would be the light, which should be visible for all to see, and the salt, seasoning and preserving the godly morals. I pray that the Forty Days for Life is the beginning of this.

You know, the Word of God makes it pretty clear just what is expected of us who believe in Jesus:

> *"What good is it, my brethren, if a man claims to have faith but has no deeds? Can such a faith save him? Suppose a brother or sister is without clothes and daily food. If one of you says to him, 'Go, I wish you well; keep warm and well fed,' but does nothing about his physical needs, what good is it? In the same way, faith by itself, if it is not accompanied by action, is dead." (James 2:14-17)*

If the Samaritan in Luke 10:30-36 had not been on the street he would not have seen the injured man. How many injured people are on the highways and streets that are going unattended and are dying?

I wonder how many of us are so busy with our Bible studies and church activities that we just casually walk by and not see the injured.

Furthermore, I find it interesting that in the Bible wisdom is found on the street! In **Proverbs 8:1-4 the Bible tells us: "Does not wisdom call out? Does not understanding raise her voice? On the heights along the way, where the paths meet, she takes her stand; beside the gates leading into the city, at the entrances, she cries aloud; To you O men, I call out; I raise my voice to all mankind."**

Are we hearing her voice as we sing on Sunday morning?

Please understand that I truly believe radio and TV evangelists, Crusades, concerts, and books, Bible studies and church attendance are all wonderful and extremely important. Yet, all too often we minister His love only to each other!

Furthermore, I praise the Lord for the awesome ministries in our country that are effectively ministering the love of Jesus to others.

What I am saying is this: the church at large needs to get out of the buildings, sacrifice some of our time and go out to pray. The truth is that pastors all over this country pray for the martyrs across the world, they pray and preach about the victims of Katrina and yet rarely the Holocaust of abortion (the worst the world has ever seen) is addressed, much less preached about! If thousands of Christians went to their local killing centers and truly prayed, how long do you think it would be before they closed? How many people do you think would be saved? How many babies? How many women and men would be helped in a practical way?

When we look at the church at large we see apathy in much larger numbers. Just think of what would happen if the body of Christ would really unite and take the stand that He has commanded us to do!

Jesus made it very clear regarding what He expected of people who believed in Him:

> *"May they be brought to complete unity to let the world know that you sent me and have loved them even as you have loved me."* (John 17:23)

Isn't it time to let the world know just how much Jesus loves everyone? Isn't it time to put aside all the petty differences, stand side by side in repentance and say, "Jesus is Lord, the killing must stop"? Why is it so hard for us to come out of the four walls of our churches and take a visible stand? What is it? Is it fear or apathy? Or just plain denial?

The definition of *apathy* according to Noah Webster is: "Want of feeling, utter privation of passion or insensibility to pain, a calmness of mind, incapable of being ruffled by pleasure, pain or passion."

Has the church in America become comfortably numb? As long as it doesn't touch our lives we can ignore what is happening? Are we all living for today and not taking notice that if we don't take a visible stand for truth now, regarding the killing of God's precious babies that it will affect our future? Are we just paying lip service to the King of Kings? Not willing to sacrifice time or energy to further His Kingdom.

The definition of *deny* is: "Neglect to acknowledge; to refuse; to contradict; to disown; to speak against. Are we all in denial because we are refusing to acknowledge pre-born babies are dying because we are not united in His love?

I have heard pastors say, "Abortion is a political issue and we can't get involved." Let's think about that. How can the deliberate killing of a pre-born baby that has come from the heart of our Father be a political issue? Rather, it is a Christian issue that needs to be addressed by the body of Christ now before it is too late.

Abortion is a symptom of a very sick society. It is not just the laws that need to change. It is the hearts of men, women and children that need to change. The law will change only after the heart has found Love again. Furthermore, isn't that our assignment here on earth?

The Dred Scott decision prior to the Civil War said black people were property! That is totally wrong, evil and there was a major war because of it. Roe v Wade says pre-born babies do not have a right to life. Doe v Bolton legalized abortion right up to labor! That is totally wrong, evil and we as the church stay relatively silent! God, forgive us and give us a chance to make it right.

Just look at the culture in our country today. Not only do we kill pre-born babies, men are now marrying men, women are marrying women. Children that are adopted have two fathers or two mothers, not a mother and a father. What effect do we think that will have on our future? The internet is effectively destroying any morals and values that still exist with the excessive amount of pornography that is on it. Liberal teachers are teaching from their own agenda and brainwashing our children. Television is corrupt, immoral and oh-so entertaining. The games our children are playing are causing emotional and physical violence. The political atmosphere is filled with so much hate and hyprocosy. I could go on and on, but the point is the church in general has been silent and it is time to wake up! We will be held accountable and no excuse will be good enough for Jesus when we stand in front of Him.

It is the touching, seeing and looking into the lost and lonely eyes of the downtrodden, with a heart full of compassion that will change this country and is what changes hearts.

I believe what Jesus said in Matthew 25:35-36, (paraphrased) "You fed the hungry, you visited the prisoner, you gave a glass of water to the thirsty, you gave clothes to the person who had none, you took care of the sick." He ended this command with; "I tell you the truth, whatever you did for the least of these brothers of mine you did for me." (vs. 40) I don't think He meant for us to wait until they walked through the door of our church!

I believe that standing up for the least (and you can't get anymore least than the little one in the womb whose voice cannot be heard) is something all Christians could do.

> *"Everyone who calls on the name of the Lord will be saved. How, then, can they call on the One they have not believed in? And how can they believe in the One of whom they have not heard? And how can they hear without someone preaching to them? And how can they preach unless they are sent? As it is written, 'How beautiful are the feet of those who bring good news!'" (Romans 10:13-15)*

That Scripture is not for church on Sunday. Nor is it just for the Pastors from the pulpit. It is for you and for me. However, there is a high price to pay for "beautiful feet." The price is a willing, humble and contrite heart. That is not easy. It hurts, yet the Lord tells us **in Psalm 51:17, "The sacrifices of God are a broken spirit; a broken and contrite heart, O God, you will not despise."**

I live in Western New York where there are about 7,000 churches. If one person from each church went to an abortion center to pray for one hour that would be seven thousand people! Yet when I go, there are times when there is no one there to stand in the gap for the little ones, whose screams no one hears.

Then there are our children. The world tells them, "Don't trust God," and we say, "Trust Him with all your heart." Kids watch, listen and imitate much more than we care to admit. And the children of today are in the valley of choice. On one side is the kingdom of darkness with all its temptations, with all the easy solutions and all its powerful and seductive role models. On the other side is the Kingdom of light with rainbows of love, security, strength and eternal life. The role models? Mom, dad, the Sunday school teacher, the youth pastor and the musical groups. If none of us have the courage of our convictions to take the moral high ground and to take a visible stand; what will they do?

Our children must be given the tools/weapons of truth by the example we set. Love is an action word; it must be expressed by giving it away. What better way than to love the innocent children being led to the slaughter?

We need to communicate with our young in a clear, exciting, interesting and informative way. There have been many times when I have taken some of my grandchildren to the abortion centers to pray, hold a sign, or even pass out literature. Their hearts caught the fire from heaven, their minds received the truth and their spirits became stronger in the Lord. Our conversations during these times were intense and positive.

We need to show our posterity, by our actions, that God can be trusted and He does answer sincere prayer. We must show them, no matter what happens to any of us, the love of Jesus our Christ is more than sufficient. By our example we set the standard and show the truth of our hope in Christ.

If we don't act in truth, if we don't stand up for truth, if we are not willing to sacrifice for Christ... why should they?

Have we noticed that men and women ordained by God to preach His Word are not respected like they used to be? Have we noticed that when Christians stands up for their belief they are mocked, and sometimes arrested for just passing out tracts? That is happening all over our country, especially in the pro-life and pro-marriage ministries.

I believe there is no danger for the person who says, "Jesus is my Savior." It is when we say, "Jesus is Lord and I must obey His Word!" the trouble begins. Yet, if the whole true body of Christ stood up, the light would be so bright the darkness would have to flee.

Real Christianity is a way of life that walks along a path of endurance. A Christian is one who is committed to being obedient to God, no matter how high the cost. Scripture tells us:

"Jesus replied, 'No one who puts his hand to the plow and

looks back is fit for service in the Kingdom of God'" (Luke 9:62)

If you have ever watched a farmer plow a field with horse or oxen, you have seen that he focuses on a point of reference at the other end of the field. He puts his eyes on that point and begins his plowing. He does not take his eyes off this point and he does not try to hurry because if he does, the furrow will become crooked. He is steadfast; committed to the straight path and focused on the point of reference.

Our point of reference is the Word of God and His Holy Spirit; the world is the field, our equipment is our faith and determination to be obedient to His will. It is vital to a committed walk with the Lord that we are steadfast and ready to endure. Then the victories will be seen.

Thomas Jefferson said, "Yes, we did produce a near perfect Republic. But will they keep it or will they, in the enjoyment of plenty, lose the memory of freedom? Material abundance without character is the surest way to destruction."

I see that happening all over our country, don't you? Our country is being destroyed from within. Isn't it time to stop the destruction?

Once again, I believe we have made great strides in the right direction. Yet, I also believe it is time for a deeper walk with our Lord and a real commitment to action. Thousands of children live because of pro-life action. Thousands of parents have received the practical help needed to make a good life. Thousands of people have received a personal relationship with Jesus because of the Christian pro-lifers. Some laws have been changed for the good and the truth is being seen; however, I believe also that we are at a crossroads in the body of Christ.

Martin Luther King, Jr. said, "We are now faced with the fact that tomorrow is today. We are confronted with the fierce urgency of now. In this unfolding cauldron of life and history, there is such a thing as being 'too late.' Procrastination is still the thief of time. Life often leaves us standing bare, naked and dejected with a lost opportunity. The tide in the affairs of men does not remain at the flood; it ebbs. We may cry out desperately for time to stop her passage. But time is deaf to every plea and rushes on. Over the bleached bones and jumbled residue are written the pathetic words, 'Too Late.' There is an invisible book of life that faithfully records our vigilance or our neglect. …'The moving finger writes, and having writ moves on…'"

Can we as His body, His ambassadors here on earth, put aside our differences and look in the same direction? Can we agree that Jesus Christ is the Lord of Lords and the shedding of innocent blood must stop?

The Cross is the way.
Our King has given us the weapons
Our King has given us the power
Our King has given us the victory!

Let us pray up, stand up, show up and together let the Light and Love of Jesus shine for the world to see! Before it is too late.